I CAN LEAD

STRONG TO CHANGE
BRAVE TO LEAD

Ayman Nassar, M.Sc.
Zain Aurangzeb Nisar, M.Sc.

Islamic Leadership Institute of America

Cover
> Photographer: Ayman Nassar
> Image: Islamic Leadership Institute of America Career Empowerment program, EmpoweReer, summer of 2025 cohort, Isaiah Hickson of Baltimore, Maryland, at Park Heights, Baltimore.
> Cover Design: Abdelrahman Abdou, Zain Nisar.

Book Team
> Author(s): Zain Nisar.
> Contributor(s): Ayman Nassar, Zain Nisar.
> Internal Design: Abdelrahman Abdou, Maria Tuvilla
> Reviewers: Abdelrahman Abdou, Ayman Nassar, Esraa Badr, Mehr Nadeem, Dr. Mohammed Wardani, and Zain Nisar.

Publisher: Islamic Leadership Institute of America, Inc.

Copyright © 2025, Islamic Leadership Institute of America, Inc.

All rights reserved. Printed in the United States of America. Except as permitted under the United States Copyright Act of 1976, no part of this publication may be reproduced or distributed in any form or by any means, or stored in a database or retrieval system, without prior written permission of the publisher.

First Edition, First Printing, October 2025 ~ Rabi Thani 1447.

ISBN-13   9798272542465

Copies of the book can be ordered through amazon.com, islamicleadership.org, and other online bookstores. Bulk order discounts are available by contacting ILIA.

> 4903 Liberty Heights Ave, Baltimore, MD 21207
> info@islamicleadership.org
> www.islamicleadership.org

Islamic Leadership Institute of America is a 501(c)3 non-profit educational and research organization dedicated to leadership development, capacity building, and community empowerment.

Islamic Leadership Institute of America, ILIA, EmpoweReer and I Can Lead are trademarks of Islamic Leadership Institute of America, Inc.

Acknowledgment

All praise and gratitude belong to the Creator of the Heavens and Earth, the Source of wisdom, mercy, and guidance. This book is a humble offering drawn from that bounty—an effort to translate lived experience into knowledge, and knowledge into hope, and hope into positive action for generations of youth who can transform their lives and contribute meaningful gifts to this nation. Whatever benefit is found within these pages is by our Creator's grace alone.

This work was developed for young people whose potential is too often overlooked, especially those navigating incarceration, system involvement, and social marginalization. Over many years, we have witnessed how access to meaningful guidance, practical leadership tools, and affirming belief can alter a young person's trajectory. This book exists because thousands of incarcerated and system-impacted youth demonstrated—through their questions, struggles, insights, and resilience—that leadership is not a privilege reserved for a few, but a responsibility and possibility for all, beginning with the simple and powerful practice of self-leadership.

I Can Lead represents the culmination of more than seventeen years of work: hundreds of workshops delivered across the United States, spanning over twelve states—from Michigan in the north to Texas in the west and Georgia in the south, and of course our home, the Free State of Maryland. These sessions took place in classrooms, juvenile detention centers, community spaces, and family settings, reaching thousands of young people and hundreds of educators, counselors, and youth workers. Every chapter carries the imprint of real lives, real challenges, and real growth observed in these spaces.

We are deeply grateful for the institutional partners who believed in the importance of this work and invested in its impact.

We acknowledge the support of Maryland's Governor Wes Moore's Office of Crime Prevention and Policy (GOCPP), Maryland's Department of Juvenile Services (DJS), and Baltimore Children and Youth Fund (BCYF) for their commitment to prevention, rehabilitation, and positive youth development. Their partnership made it possible to bring evidence-informed, values-driven leadership education to young people who need it most as part of their reentry. We are also grateful to the support of our Baltimore City's 8th District Councilmember, Mr. Paris Gray, and 41st District Delegate, Mr. Sean A. Stinnett for their support and encouragement of youth development across the city. Lastly, and not least we would be remiss to not mention Mrs. Shauntia Lindsey, Statewide Program Services Coordinator for Residential Services at DJS, and Mr. Keon Chavez, Business Services Representative, at Mayor's Office on Employment and Development, both who have been the spark to all this impactful reentry work.

We also extend heartfelt thanks to our community and to all individuals and organizations who funded, supported, and sustained Islamic Leadership Institute of America (ILIA), and its Juvenile Empowerment Program (JEP) over the years. Your trust and generosity enabled consistent presence, long-term engagement, and the patience required to do this work with integrity rather than haste. Our organization continues to dedicate its mission to serving all youth, regardless of their faith, to become empowered to make a positive lasting impact on themselves and their communities, discovering and fulfilling their purpose as humans.

This book would not exist without the dedication of our academic contributors and our positive youth development research team. Their rigor ensured that lived experience was matched with sound theory, ethical practice, and research-based frameworks. Together, they helped translate years of fieldwork into a resource that educators, mentors, and youth can rely on with confidence.

Finally, we acknowledge our families. Their patience, sacrifice, and quiet encouragement sustained the long hours, travel, and emotional labor that this work demanded. Behind every workshop, late night, and difficult conversation was a network of loved ones who believed in the mission even when the outcomes were not yet visible.

May this book serve as a means of growth, dignity, and possibility for every young person who encounters it—and may it stand as a reminder that when knowledge is paired with compassion and opportunity, transformation is not only possible, but inevitable.

Ayman and Zain

TABLE OF CONTENTS

01. IDENTITY BUILDING: WHO AM I? — 19

Activity 1: What Does Identity Mean to You? — 20
Activity 2: My Identity Blueprint — 25
Activity 3: Write Your Autobiography — 27
Activity 4: Self-Check: My Identity Traits — 28

02. MISSION & PURPOSE: WHAT AM I ALL ABOUT? — 33

Activity 1: My Life Ingredients — 34
Activity 2: Drafting My Mission Statement — 41
Activity 3: My 1–2 Year Vision Roadmap — 42

03. VISION: MY MAP TO THE FUTURE — 45

Activity 1: Painting My Life's Picture — 48
Activity 2: Facing My Challenges — 51
Activity 3: My Personal Vision Statement — 52
Activity 4: My Roadmap for the Next 1–2 Years — 53

04. PROBLEM SOLVING FOR TEENS & YOUNG ADULTS — 55

Activity 1: What Is the Real Problem? — 57
Activity 2: 5 Whys Exercise — 62
Activity 3: Fishbone Diagram: What's Really Causing the Problem? — 63
Activity 4: Zoom In – Scope Your Focus — 65
Activity 5: SMART Goal Builder — 66
Activity 6: Reflect and Grow — 67

05. PATIENCE, PERSEVERANCE & STEADFASTNESS — 71

Activity 1: Trigger Tracker – When I Want to Quit — 73
Activity 2: My Perseverance Contract — 76

TABLE OF CONTENTS

06. TIME MANAGEMENT: SMART HUSTLE — 79

- Activity 1: Time Audit – Where Does My Time Go? — 81
- Activity 2: The Power Hour – Start Your Day With Purpose — 85
- Activity 3: Balance Check – The 5-Part Wheel — 88
- Activity 4: Design Your Weekly Plan — 89

07. SUBMISSION: LEARNING TO LET GO AND LEAN IN — 93

- Activity 1: Where Do You Push, Where Do You Flow? — 95
- Activity 2: Submission Strength Builder — 97

08. PURIFICATION: CLEARING THE JUNK SO YOU CAN LEAD — 99

- Activity 1: Clean Start — 101
- Activity 2: Trash Out — 101
- Activity 3: Scenario Check — 102
- Activity 4: My Purification Action Plan — 103

09. COMMUNICATION: SAY IT CLEAR, SAY IT REAL — 105

- Activity 1: First Impressions — 107
- Activity 2: The Stuck Student — 107
- Activity 3: Feedback Request — 108
- Activity 4: Message Makeover — 109

10. COMMUNICATING WITH ADULTS: MAKE THE CLICK, BRIDGE THE GAP (FAMILY) — 111

- Activity 1: Communication Iceberg — 113
- Activity 2: Communication Style Check — 118
- Activity 3: Pause Before You Speak — 119
- Activity 4: Respectful Comebacks — 120

11. SELF-AWARENESS: ACING MY GAME — 123

- Activity 1: My Emotion Tracker — 125
- Activity 2: My Strengths and Growth Areas — 127
- Activity 3: Leadership Self-Check Quiz — 130
- Activity 4: "Pause and Choose" Scenarios — 131
- Activity 5: "My Daily Check-In Template — 134

TABLE OF CONTENTS

12. ANGER MANAGEMENT: TURNING HEAT INTO POWER — 137

- Activity 1: My Anger Signals — 139
- Activity 2: Reframe the Scene — 140
- Activity 3: Two Columns — 141
- Activity 4: My Anger Plan — 142

13. RISK ANALYSIS & SMART CHOICE: FINE LINE BETWEEN COURAGE & STUPIDITY — 145

- Activity 1: Risk Reflection Map — 147
- Activity 2: Courage or Careless? — 148
- Activity 3: My SMART Decision Chart — 151
- Activity 4: Pros & Cons Chart – What's the Real Choice? — 152
- Activity 5: My Risk Wisdom Toolkit — 156

14. RIGHTS AND OBLIGATIONS — 159

- Activity 1: Rights & Responsibilities Match — 160
- Activity 2: Everyday Rights Check — 162
- Activity 3: My Role, My Responsibility — 163
- Activity 4: Step Into Their Shoes — 165
- Activity 5: My Citizenship Plan — 167

15. WEALTH & PATIENCE: BUILDING WITHOUT BREAKING — 169

- Activity 1: My Wealth List — 171
- Activity 2: $100 Challenge — 171
- Activity 3: Wealth Builder Plan — 172

16. FAIRNESS: PLAYING IT STRAIGH — 175

- Activity 1: My Fair & Unfair Moments — 177
- Activity 2: Role-Play — 179
- Activity 3: My Fairness Pledge — 180

17. RESUME WRITING: TELLING YOUR STORY ON PAPER — 183

- Activity 1: Resume Inventory Sheet — 185
- Activity 2: Match the Job — 186
- Activity 3: Resume Do-Over — 187
- Activity 4: Build Your First Resume Draft — 188

TABLE OF CONTENTS

18. JOB HUNTING: FINDING YOUR FIRST OPPORTUNITY — 191

- Activity 1: My Job Map — 193
- Activity 2: Role-Play — 194
- Activity 3: My Network List — 194

19. LEARNING: NEVER STOP GROWING — 197

- Activity 1: Hidden Lessons — 199
- Activity 2: Mindset Check — 200
- Activity 3: Listening Practice — 201
- Activity 4: Strong Questions — 203
- Activity 5: Learning-to-Action Plan — 204

20. BASICS OF THINKING: SHARPENING YOUR MIND — 207

- Activity 1: React vs. Reflect — 209
- Activity 2: Debate Both Sides — 210
- Activity 3: Thinking Sampler — 212
- Activity 4: Five Whys — 213

21. VOCATIONAL FOUNDATIONS: LEADING WITH YOUR HANDS — 217

- Activity 1: Job Sort — 219
- Activity 2: Skill Hunt — 220
- Activity 3: Mini Debate — 221
- Activity 4: My Trade Path Checklist — 222

22. PERFORMANCE: TURNING EFFORT INTO RESULTS — 225

- Activity 1: Effort and Results — 227
- Activity 2: Success Check — 228
- Activity 3: Mini-Project Plan — 229
- Activity 4: Create a Tracker — 230
- Activity 5: Scenario Talk — 231

23. I CAN LEAD: MY LEADERSHIP LEGACY — 235

- Activity 1: My Legacy Story — 239
- Activity 2: Legacy Brainstorm — 239
- Activity 3: My Leadership Legacy Statementr — 240

My Lord! Open my heart, ease my task for me; loosen a knot from my tongue, that they may understand my saying.

– Prophet Moses as he transforms Egypt. Quran, Surah Taha (20:25-28)

PREFACE

Mistakes are inevitable. We all make mistakes. We are human!

That is really important to remember, because we are human, if we use our minds properly and make the right decisions in life, we would be elevated higher than angels. If we make wrong decisions we become worse than animals and beasts.

Humans are a very unique species.

They have a powerful organ, more powerful than a supercomputer, more flexible than a slinky. It can expand and contract just like your muscles, depending how much practice you give it, through reading, learning and exploring. It can grow and strengthen just like going to the gym, depending on much training, awareness and care you provide it. It is our brain.

Smart humans are those who learn from past experiences. Past experiences can be positive or negative, or perceived as either, we might not even know. What we do know is that our Creator knows everything, including what is in our hearts. He knows our intentions, dreams and aspirations.

Make a promise to yourself to purify your intentions, by forgiving others, loving everyone, caring for yourself and making the right decisions.

It all starts with a sincere, pure intention.

An intention to change through strength, and the courage to pull through.

PLEDGE

I _____ pledge on this day to commit to my personal growth and the growth of my community. I promise to learn from past experiences and to be inspired to explore new ideas, opportunities and to be curious about the world and my purpose in it.

I realize there are pure and wounded parts to my being and that as a human, I need to nurture both my body and soul.

I look forward to using my humanity in making the world a better place for all, and to discover my purpose and the reason for me being on planet earth.

I will bring more light, peace, love and hope to this world through my personal journey of self-reflection, healing, learning and self-leadership.

I will reach out to trusted caregivers to help me through my journey in life, and will share with those who need my help and guidance. I will be part of a larger ecosystem of humans.

_____   _____
Signature   Today's Date

INTRODUCTION

Are You Ready to Lead?

Maybe a teacher handed you this book because they see something special in you. Maybe you picked it up because you're curious about leadership. Either way, welcome. I'm glad you're here.

Leadership begins with small choices: helping a friend, speaking up when something's wrong, or planning a group project. To explore what leadership looks like, consider a **slinky** and a **pencil**:

- A slinky stretches and then returns to its shape. You can pull it apart and it bounces back. If you stretch it too far, it twists or breaks.
- A pencil is strong and makes its mark. But if you try to bend it, it snaps.

Some leaders are like slinkies. They adapt when things change. They stay calm under pressure. They know how to bounce back. Others are like pencils. They might look tough, but if they never listen or adjust, they can break under stress.

This book will help you become a leader who is strong and flexible, like a slinky. You'll learn how to face tough situations, recover from mistakes, and lead with kindness.

Young Leaders Make Big Differences

Leadership isn't about age. Throughout history, teens have started movements, created projects, and sparked change in their communities. Maybe you know someone your age who organized a park cleanup or started a mental health awareness campaign. They didn't wait until they were adults. They saw a need and stepped up.

You don't need to know everything or hold a title. All you need is the willingness to learn, grow, and act. This book will guide you through skills like communicating, solving problems, using your time wisely, and making smart decisions.

Why Now? Why You?

You already have something valuable: your voice and your choices. People notice how you act and how you handle challenges. You can lead by example right now.

Your First Challenge: Be Honest With Yourself

Ask yourself:

- When do I snap under pressure like a pencil?
- When do I bend too much and lose sight of who I am?
- When do I bounce back like a slinky?

You don't have to be perfect. You just have to try. Leadership is about kindness, clear boundaries, growth, and impact. You don't need to be the loudest in the room to make a difference. It starts with small steps and honest reflection.

REFLECTION TIME

Take a moment to think or write about:

- Which thing you feel like right now—a slinky, a pencil, or something else.

  _____
  _____
  _____

- A time you bounced back after a challenge.

  _____
  _____
  _____

- A way you want to grow as a leader this year.

  _____
  _____
  _____

A Place to Grow

Do you have big dreams? Maybe you want to start a business, get into a certain school, or simply find out what you're good at. I Can Lead is here to help you do that. This six-month program is more than just a class. It's a journey where you'll learn real-life leadership skills, explore your goals, try new things, and build something you're proud of.

THE PROGRAM

What You Will Learn

By the end of the program, you will:

- **Lead projects and people with confidence.**
- **Communicate clearly**, whether you're speaking in class, at work, or in an interview.
- **Solve real problems**, not just on paper but in everyday situations.
- **Manage your time and feelings** so you can stay organized and calm.
- **Take charge of your growth** by setting goals and following through.
- **Create a project that matters** to you and the people around you.

You won't have to do any of this alone. Mentors, teammates, and a supportive community will be with you every step of the way.

CAREER TRACKS

HOW IT WORKS

YOUR LEARNING JOURNERY

Here's how the program works:

1. **Apply and Enroll** – Fill out a simple form to join.
2. **Join a Group** – Within a month, you'll be placed in a cohort with other students.
3. **Work on Real Projects** – A few times a week, you'll meet with a coach and tackle projects that build leadership and life skills.
4. **Share Your Project** – Later, you'll enter your project in a friendly competition for a chance to earn a cash prize.
5. **Plan Your Future** – Choose a path that fits your goals: getting a job, continuing your education, starting a business, or learning a trade. Your coach will help you with résumés, interviews, and planning. Support will continue for up to a year after the program.

WELCOME TO I CAN LEAD

I CAN LEAD
A Young Adult Leadership-Based Reentry Program

CAREER TRACK & LAUNCH
Your coach will support your career plan, and you can choose from one of 4 tracks; *employment, school, entrepreneurship or trade*. You will also receive coaching and help with job interviews for up to a year.

COMPETITION
You can continue in the program when you go back home, and will have a chance to join a project competition. Top three contestants of your cohort win up to $1000!

REAL-LIFE PROJECT EXPERIENCE
You will meet with your coach a few tiems a week and engage in various leadership development activities

LEARNING JOURNEY
You will be assigned a cohort within 30 days

LEAD YOU
JUMPSTART YOUR CAREER

ADMISSION & ENROLLMENT
Complete a short form (see reverse side), and get your case manager approval.

What You Need to Do

To complete the program successfully:

1. **Complete a work personality assessment** to learn about your work style.
2. **Create a plan** with your coach.
3. **Attend at least 90 percent** of the sessions.
4. **Finish all assignments and projects.**
5. **Use what you learn** in a real project of your choice.
6. **Choose one of the four tracks** – job, trade school, college or entrepreneurship.
7. **Score at least 80 percent** on the final test.

Your effort and commitment will help you make the most of this experience and set you up for success beyond the program.

TRADE

EMPLOYMENT

COLLEGE

ENTREPRENEURSHIP

1

Identity Building
Who Am I?

Who Am I, Really?

Take a second and ask yourself:

- Who am I?
- Beyond my name, my username, or the roles other people give me—what makes me, *me*?

You might be someone people turn to when things fall apart. Maybe you're the quiet observer who watches and listens before speaking. Maybe you love solving problems or dreaming up big ideas. We all wear different hats every day—student, sibling, athlete, artist. But your **identity** goes deeper. It's your inner compass. It helps you figure out what matters, how you handle tough moments, and how you lead.

ACTIVITY 1.1

What Does Identity Mean to You?

Instructions: In your own words, answer the question: "What does identity mean to me?" Go beyond labels like student, gamer, or athlete. Think about your values, personality, and goals. Write 3–5 sentences below:

Write here (3–5 sentences):

_____
_____
_____
_____

Why Identity Matters

Here's a simple idea: **how you see yourself shapes how you act**. Think of it this way:

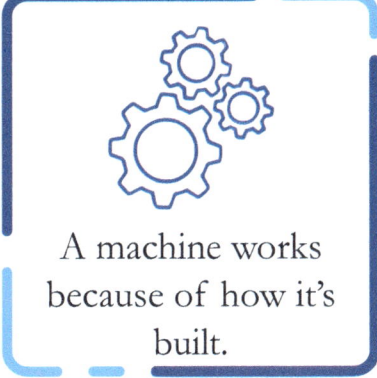
A machine works because of how it's built.

A team functions because of the rules it follows.

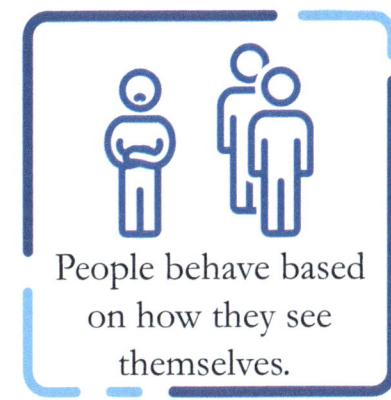
People behave based on how they see themselves.

If you believe you're just average, you might not take risks. If you see yourself as a leader, you'll look for ways to help others. Your identity influences your goals, relationships, and how you show up in the world.

LEADERSHIP IN ACTION

Think about someone like Greta Thunberg, Malala Yousafzai, or another young person who knows what they stand for. They didn't just say *what* they were. They were clear about *why* they speak up, *who* they want to be, and *how* they plan to live. Malala knew education mattered, so she spoke out even when it was risky. Greta speaks about climate action with clarity and purpose. Dr. Martin Luther King is another great example. He had a dream and was clear about why it mattered.

You should not let others define you, but rather you promote your identity to others …

Here's what I stand for.

Here's how I plan to live.

Here's what I care about.

…these are powerful assertions. That's identity.

What Makes Up a Strong Identity?

A strong identity isn't about being perfect. It's about knowing yourself, being honest about your values, walking the talk and trying to grow. Some traits that help build a strong character are:

Clear Purpose

Knowing what matters to you and why you care.

Self-Awareness

Understanding your strengths and where you struggle.

Guidance

Learning from wise people and pausing to think before you act.

Humility

Keeping ego in check and staying open to growth.

Patience

Staying calm when life gets frustrating, and enduring annoyance.

Consistency

Sticking to your values, even when it's hard.

Sincerity

Being real, even when no one's watching.

Responsibility

Owning your actions and learning from mistakes.

Compassion

Treating others with kindness and empathy.

Curiosity

Asking questions and seeking understanding.

Thoughtfulness

Reflecting, thinking, coming up with ideas before reacting.

Perseverance

Keeping at it when its tough, and not just annoying, but also painful.

Integrity

Staying true to your principles.

Confidence

Believing in your ability to make a difference.

Growth mindset

Aiming for progress rather than perfection.

You don't have to master all of these today. Practicing them a little at a time will strengthen your identity and earn you trust and respect.

Real-World Identity = Real-World Leadership

Knowing who you are isn't just about "self-awareness." It affects how you:

- Make choices when the pressure's on.
- Speak up (or stay silent) when something feels wrong.
- Step up to lead when others are unsure.
- Set boundaries and stay grounded in your values.

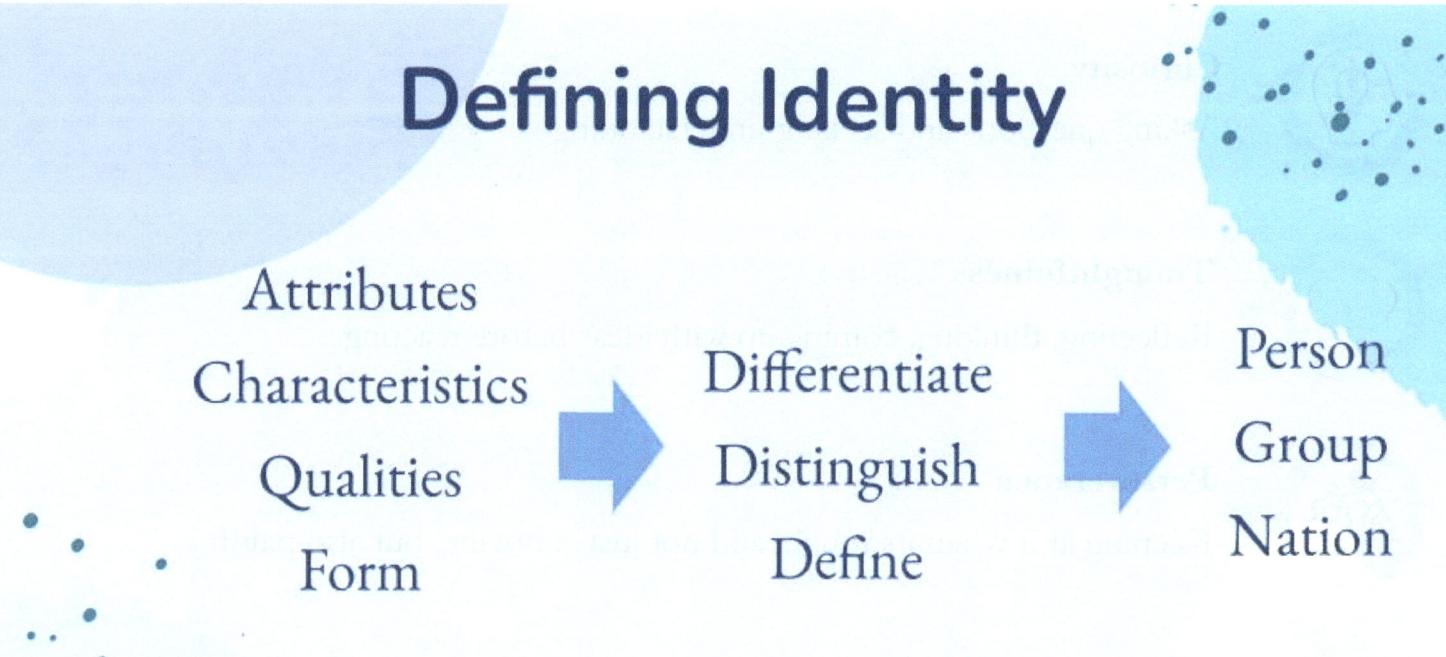

Defining identity starts with understanding the attributes, characteristics, qualities, form or structure of a person. Identity is what makes us diverse and different, hence we identify as individual, groups or nations.

Think about which groups you associate with, and how you bring diversity to the world.

People with strong identities don't just blend in. They show up with purpose.

My Identity Blueprint

Instructions: Fill in these sections to map out your identity. Think deeply about what shapes who you are:

- **Background** (Where I come from):
  _____
  _____
  _____

- **Current Situation** (What life looks like now):
  _____
  _____
  _____

- **Interests/Passions**: (What do I enjoy doing?)
  _____
  _____
  _____

- **Beliefs** (What I know to be true):
  _____
  _____
  _____

- **Personal Values** (What matters most to me):
  _____
  _____
  _____

ACTIVITY 1.2

ACTIVITY 1.2 CONTINUED

- What I'm still figuring out:
  _____
  _____
  _____
  _____
  _____

Understanding Me & Drafting My Bio

Name	I am Huda,...
Age	...12 years old,...
Relationships	...have 3 siblings and live with my parents,...
Accomplishments	...I completed sixth grade last year, and also earned a girls scout badge, and a certificate in robotics...
Current Situation	...currently I am a student at Greater Lansing Islamic School,...
Beliefs	... I believe learning history is very important, so we can learn from the experiences of previous nations, and avoid their mistakes, as well as learn from the successes.
Interests	... I like math, basketball, Quran and to go camping with my cousins,...
Other Relevant	...I look forward to being a business leader, applying Islam so people are not suffering from poverty.

A biography is an overview of a person, their identity, background, relationship to a group or entity, some of their major accomplishments that make them unique and special in the world, as well as their values, beliefs, interests and other relevant information to the people they are connecting with.

Write Your Autobiography

Instructions: Imagine someone asked you to introduce yourself—not by name or role, but by your purpose, values, and character. Write a 4–6 sentence autobiography that reflects the real you.

Use these sentence starters if helpful:

- *I am someone who…*
- *I try to live by the value of…*
- *I want to be remembered for…*
- *I believe my purpose is to…*
- *I am working on…*

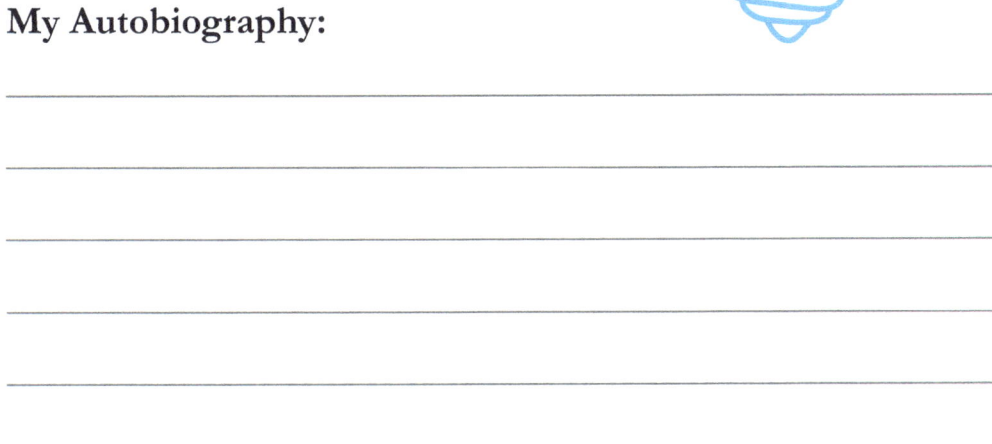

My Autobiography:

_____

_____

_____

_____

_____

_____

ACTIVITY 1.3

Self-Check: My Identity Trait

Instructions: Below is a list of identity-building traits. Place a ✓ in the box that best describes you. You may check more than one box per row if both apply.

Trait	I Practice This Often	I'm Still Working on This	This Describes Me Best
Clear Purpose			
Self-Aware			
Guided			
Humble			
Patient			
Consistent			
Sincere			
Responsible			
Compassionate			
Inquisitive			
Thinker			
Hard Working			
Strong			
Powerful			
Seeks Perfection			

ACTIVITY 1.4

ACTIVITY 1.4 CONTINUED

Pick one trait you checked under "I'm Still Working on This." Write one thing you can do to grow in that area this month.

_____
_____
_____
_____
_____

Identity isn't something you find once and keep forever. It's something you build, protect, and refine as you grow. The more clearly you understand who you are and what you stand for, the stronger and clearer your leadership becomes.

LEADERSHIP IN ACTION

Meet Diego. He used to act different depending on the group he was with. Around his loud friends, he pretended to be tough. Around teachers, he played the quiet kid. Deep down, he felt like nobody really knew the real him.

One day, a mentor asked him, *"What do you actually care about?"*

He thought about it and wrote down three values: **loyalty, honesty, and creativity**. From then on, he tried to live by those values no matter where he was. At first it felt hard—he worried people wouldn't like the "real" him. But over time, his friends and teachers started to respect him more.

Why? Because he wasn't switching masks anymore. He was being himself. His identity gave him strength.

REFLECTION TIME

- What do I see when I look at the mirror?

　
　
　

- What values do I want to guide my decisions (honesty, loyalty, kindness, creativity…)?

　
　
　

- When I face pressure, do I usually act more like myself—or more like what others expect?

THINK ABOUT IT

1. A classmate is being teased for being different. Do you stay quiet, join in, or speak up? What does your choice say about your identity?

   _____
   _____
   _____

2. You get invited to skip class with friends, but you know it goes against your values. How do you respond?

   _____
   _____
   _____

3. Someone compliments you for being smart, but you don't feel confident inside. How can you act in line with your true identity instead of how others label you?

   _____
   _____
   _____

4. Imagine you're in charge of a small project at school. How would knowing your strengths and values help you lead?

   _____
   _____
   _____

Mission & Purpose
What Am I All About?

Why Ask "Why?"

Let's get deep for a second: **Why are you here? Why were you created?**

That question feels huge—and it's supposed to. Knowing your **mission** (what you want to dedicate your life to) and **purpose** (why you want to do that) is like having a compass. When you understand these two things, life makes more sense. You stop drifting and start steering. You stop reacting and start leading.

ACTIVITY 2.1

My Life Ingredients

Instructions: List the top five things that matter most to you right now. These can be values (like honesty), causes (like mental health), or dreams (like starting a community garden). Then explain why each one matters to you. Once you are done, use this list to guide the focus of your mission.

	What I Care About Most	Why It Matters to Me
1		
2		
3		
4		
5		

Mission vs. Purpose

Here's one way to think about it:

 **Mission** is your passion. It answers:

What am I here to do?
How do I want to impact the world?
What do I want to dedicate my life for?

VS

 **Purpose** is your motivation reason. It answers:

Why does this matter to me?
What deeper meaning drives me every day?

Together, your mission and purpose shape your mindset, your decisions, and your goals.

Why You Need Mission & Purpose?

Without mission and purpose, life can feel aimless. You might spend your time trying to fit in, please everyone, or just go with the flow. A clear mission and purpose give your life meaning. They help you:

- Make better decisions.
- Focus on what truly matters.
- Bounce back stronger from challenges.
- Live like a leader—not just hope to become one.
- Reinforces your identity, making you a stronger person in the face of life's challenges.

This Isn't About Fame

You don't have to change the entire world to live with purpose. Some people lead countries. Some lead classrooms. Some lead by being a kind friend. What matters is that you lead with intention. Your mission doesn't have to be loud; it just has to be **real**.

Goals vs. Mission

A goal is a specific result you want to achieve (like "get into college"). Your mission is the larger path you're walking ("use knowledge to help others"). Your purpose is the reason behind it all ("make the world a little better than you found it").

Goals come and go. Your mission stays with you—guiding your goals and helping you make decisions.

REFLECTION TIME

For each question, write 2–4 sentences. Be honest with yourself.

1. What are my natural gifts or strengths? (skills, personality traits, interests)

_____
_____
_____

2. What kind of person do I want to become?

_____
_____
_____

3. Who do I want to help or serve most in my life?

_____
_____
_____

4. What three qualities do I want people to remember about me?

_____
_____
_____

Meaning Beyond Yourself

Many people find energy in believing they are part of something bigger—like a community, a cause, their family, or the planet. Whether you're inspired by your faith, your culture, your passion for justice, or your love for nature, connecting your mission to something larger can give you strength and direction. The important part is to **live with purpose and lead with intention**.

Mission-Driven Lives: Then and Now

History and everyday life are full of people who didn't just dream big; they lived it:

Martin Luther King Jr.

Martin Luther King Jr. painted a picture of racial equality and worked tirelessly toward it.

Brittany Young

Brittany Young is a Baltimore native who founded the nonprofit B-360 to channel local dirt-bike culture into STEM education and career pathways.

Malala Yousafzai

Malala Yousafzai risked her life to fight for girls' education and continues to be a global voice for change.

Harriet Tubman

Harriet Tubman risked everything to help enslaved people escape to freedom.

Greta Thunberg

Greta Thunberg started with a solitary school strike and sparked a worldwide climate movement.

What makes their missions powerful? They were clear, courageous, committed, and compassionate.

You don't need to be famous to be mission-driven. A teacher starting a neighborhood reading program, a friend organizing a local cleanup, or a teenager advocating for mental health awareness are all mission-driven leaders too.

LEADERSHIP IN ACTION

Aaliyah always said she wanted to "make a difference," but she wasn't sure how. She tried sports, clubs, and even starting a YouTube channel. None of it felt real.

One night, she thought about what mattered most to her. She realized she loved helping younger kids who struggled with reading. That became her **mission**: to use her patience and creativity to help kids succeed.

At first, she only tutored one neighbor. But soon, more kids came. Within a year, she had a small reading group every Saturday. Aaliyah wasn't famous. She wasn't on TV. But she was living her purpose—and it gave her confidence and direction.

Things to Think About

What do you want to be remembered for?

What are you willing to struggle for?

What keeps you going when things get tough?

The Power of Systems

Knowing your mission is one thing; **living it** is another. That's where systems—routines, habits, and plans—come in. They help you turn good intentions into action. For example:

Daily Journal
A short daily journal to reflect on your decisions.

Weekly Schedule
A weekly schedule that includes time for helping others and resting.

Mentor or Friend
A mentor or friend who checks in with you.

Habit
A habit of placing your values before distractions.

Systems don't make you perfect; they help you make progress.

Leading Through Real-Life Struggles

Modern teens face real pressures:

Feeling lost or unmotivated.

Being afraid to stand out.

Comparing yourself to everyone else.

Wondering if you're "enough."

These feelings are **normal**. Strong leaders don't pretend they don't struggle. They:

- Don't quit when things get tough.
- Don't fake confidence they don't feel.
- Look for meaning beyond themselves.
- Keep showing up—even when it's hard.

Mindsets That Build Purpose and Strength

1. **Believe Your Life Has Meaning**
You're not random. Your time here counts. Believe that your life matters and act like it.

2. **Effort Over Perfection**
It's okay to stumble. What matters is that you keep going. Progress is more important than perfection.

3. **Gratitude Builds Confidence**
Remember how far you've come. Even small wins can boost your confidence and remind you that you're growing.

Write Your Mission. Then Live It.

A mission statement is more than a catchy quote. It's your personal compass. It should answer:

- Who am I?
- What do I care about?
- How will I lead?

You can come back to it when life gets messy. It helps you stay on track, even when no one is watching.

Drafting My Mission Statement

Instructions: Use one of these sentence starters to craft a short, real, and powerful mission statement. Pick one and finish it in your own words.

Sentence Starters (pick one):

- *"I want to live with purpose by…"*
- *"My mission is to…"*
- *"I care about making a difference through…"*

Example:

"My mission is to use my creativity and compassion to build safe spaces where people feel seen."

Now you try: Write your mission statement here.

_____

_____

_____

ACTIVITY 2.2

Create Your "Purpose Card"

Make a small card (paper or digital) that you can keep with you. Include:

- Your mission statement.
- A quote or saying that inspires you.
- A reminder like: "I was made for more" or "Purpose over pressure."

BONUS ACTIVITY

ACTIVITY 2.3

My 1-2 Year Vision Roadmap

Instructions: Now that you have your mission, turn it into action. What steps can you take over the next 1–2 years that align with your mission?

Goal	How It Connects to My Mission	Timeline
1		
2		
3		
4		
5		

Having a mission and purpose doesn't require fame or fortune. It means knowing what matters to you and acting on it. When you connect your actions to a bigger purpose—whether it's your family, community, planet, or personal beliefs—you become the kind of leader others want to follow.

THINK ABOUT IT

- What do you want to be remembered for?

  _____
  _____
  _____

- What are you willing to struggle for?

  _____
  _____
  _____

- What keeps you going when things get tough?

  _____
  _____
  _____

3

Vision
My Map to the Future

Why Vision Matters

Let's be honest: figuring out your future can feel overwhelming. There's pressure from school, family, social media, and your own expectations. With so many voices telling you what to do, it's easy to feel lost.
That's where **vision** comes in.

Your vision is a clear picture of the future you want to create. It's not just about choosing a career. It's about who you want to become, what you care about, and how you'll make a positive impact on the world.

A strong vision gives you something to hold on to when life feels shaky. It helps you stay focused when you're unsure which way to go.

More Than Just a Dream

Vision isn't daydreaming. It's deciding. It's committing to move forward—even when you're not sure of every step.

Four ingredients turn hope into action:

Purpose
Why does this matter to you?

Beliefs
What truths guide you?

Values
What do you stand for?

Passions
What lights you up?

When you bring these together, your vision stops being a wish and starts becoming a plan.

Vision in Real Life: Then and Now

History is full of young people who saw beyond their present and worked toward a better future:

Martin Luther King Jr.

Martin Luther King Jr. spoke about justice and equality. His "I Have a Dream" speech painted a clear vision of a fairer world.

Mahatma Gandhi

Mahatma Gandhi believed in peaceful resistance. His vision inspired millions to stand up without violence.

Malala Yousafzai

Malala Yousafzai championed education for girls. Even after being attacked, she returned to school and used her voice for change.

Greta Thunberg

Greta Thunberg turned her concern for the climate into a global movement. She started with a simple school strike and encouraged young people to speak up.

What made their visions powerful? They were **clear, courageous, committed**, and **compassionate**.

Clarity
They knew exactly what they stood for

Courage
They faced problems with bravery and determination

Commitment
They did not lose sight of their goal

Compassion
Their goal was always to help and pull others up

Are You Holding the Brush?

Imagine your life as a canvas and your choices as brushstrokes.

Are you painting your own picture?
Or are you letting others decide what your future looks like?

It's fine to listen to advice, but if your vision is only what others expect, it might be time to take the brush back.

ACTIVITY 3.1

Painting My Life's Picture

Instructions: Reflect on your current life. Who is holding the brush? Are you painting your own picture, or are you letting others make the choices?

List three people or things that influence your decisions right now:

1. _____
2. _____
3. _____

Reflect: Are these influences guiding me towards my true vision, or away from it? Why?

_____
_____
_____

Decision: What is one step you can take to start painting your own picture more clearly?

_____
_____

ACTIVITY 3.1 CONTINUED

Start with Where You Are

Before you map your future, be honest about the present. Ask yourself:
- *Why do I think I'm here?*
- *What excites me?*
- *What values guide my decisions?*
- *Who inspires me?*
- *What does success mean to me?*

Knowing where you stand helps you see where to go next.

What's in Your Way?

Vision is exciting, but it's not always easy. You might face:

Peer pressure

Feeling like you have to fit in.

Fear of failure

Worrying about making mistakes.

Uncertainty

Not knowing how to start or what path to take.

Every great leader faced these feelings. They moved forward by leaning on inner strengths like:

Trust in your purpose	**Patience**	**Confidence with humility**	**Forgiveness**
Knowing your "why" keeps you steady.	Understanding that change takes time.	Believing in yourself while staying open to learning.	Letting go of the past hurts so you can grow.

These aren't superpowers. They're traits you can develop, starting today.

- Who inspires me?
- What does success mean to me?

Knowing where you stand helps you see where to go next.

Facing My Challenges

Instructions: List three challenges that could hold you back. For each, pick one trait that would help you overcome it, and explain why.

Four traits you can choose from:

1. Trust in your purpose:
2. Patience & self-control
3. Self-confidence (with humility)
4. Mercy & forgiveness

Challenge	Trait That Will Help Me Most	Why This Trait?

Reflection Prompt:

Pick the trait you need to strengthen first. Write one step you can take this month to develop it further.

Trait to Strengthen: _____

My Step to Improve:

_____

_____

_____

ACTIVITY 3.2

LEADERSHIP IN ACTION

Jayden wanted to be a pro basketball player. That was his dream. But when he realized he wasn't the tallest or the fastest, he felt stuck.

A coach asked him, "What do you actually want your future to look like?" After thinking, Jayden realized what he really wanted was to inspire younger kids through sports. Even if he never went pro, he could coach, train, and motivate others. Once his vision shifted, everything clicked. He wasn't chasing a fantasy anymore—he was painting a future he could actually build.

ACTIVITY 3.3

My Personal Vision Statement

Instructions: Write one or two sentences that capture the future you want to build and the person you want to become. Be clear, be bold, and be you.

My Vision Statement:

_____

_____

_____

_____

_____

_____

My Roadmap for the Next 1-2 Years

Instructions: List five specific, achievable goals that support your vision. Be clear and realistic.

Goal Number	My Clear, Specific Goal for the Next 1–2 Years
1	
2	
3	
4	
5	

Reflect: Which of these goals am I most excited about, and why?

_____
_____
_____

Creating a vision isn't about predicting every detail of your future. It's about knowing who you are, what you stand for, and what you want to work toward. When your vision is rooted in purpose and values, it becomes a powerful compass. This compass guides you through uncertainty and helps you lead with confidence and compassion.

ACTIVITY 3.4

REFLECTION TIME

- What's one picture of my future that excites me the most?
  _____
  _____

- What fears or doubts make it hard to imagine my future?
  _____
  _____

- Who do I know (famous or not) that inspires me because they lived with vision?
  _____
  _____

THINK ABOUT IT

A parent wants you to follow a certain career path, but your vision is different. How do you respond?
_____
_____

Your friends don't take your dreams seriously and make fun of them. Do you shrink back or stay focused?
_____
_____

You keep failing at one step toward your vision. Do you give up, adjust your plan, or keep pushing?
_____
_____

Problem Solving for Teens & Young Adults

Why Problems Matter

Life throws a lot at you. Some problems are small, like losing your phone charger or dealing with a sibling who won't leave you alone. Others feel much bigger—stress about school, arguments with friends, or uncertainty about the future.

Here's something most people don't realize: a problem doesn't have to be a bad thing. It can be an opportunity to learn, grow, and lead. Leaders see problems as a chance to step up and make things better.

What Is a Problem?

In leadership (and in life), a problem is simply something that isn't okay and needs to change. You're not powerless in that moment. You can:

- Notice when something's off.
- Understand it deeply.
- Take steps to fix it.

That ability is what makes you a leader.

What Is the Real Problem?

Instructions: Think of a challenge you or your peers face at school, at home, or in your community. Write a brief problem statement, then rewrite it using the strong structure: clear, specific, and convincing.

Example:

- **Weak:** "Nobody listens to me at home."
- **Strong:** "When I speak at home, I often get interrupted or dismissed. This makes me feel ignored and less confident, and it affects how I express myself outside the house."

_____
_____
_____
_____

ACTIVITY 4.1

Obstacles vs. Problems

An **obstacle** is a quick block in your way. Sometimes you can ignore it or work around it. **A problem** is a deeper issue that needs attention, thought, and planning.

For example:

- Obstacle: The internet lags for a few minutes.
- Problem: You never finish homework on time because you're always distracted.

Obstacles slow you down. Problems teach you how to step up.

Obstacles vs. Problems: Why Problem Solving Is a Leadership Skill

Strong problem-solvers:

- Make better decisions.
- Take responsibility.
- Build trust with others
- Gain confidence when things are uncertain..

Leaders don't wait for someone else to fix things. They ask themselves, "What can I do right now to move things in a better direction?"

LEADERSHIP IN ACTION

Jamal kept getting detention because he was always late. At first, he blamed the teachers, saying, "They're too strict." But after a mentor challenged him to look deeper, Jamal realized the real problem wasn't the teachers—it was his morning routine.

He never laid out clothes the night before. He always hit snooze. He wasted time looking for his shoes. Once he fixed those habits, he stopped being late. The lesson? Leaders solve the real problem, not just the surface one.

Learning from Leaders

Many great leaders—activists, thinkers, and everyday heroes—didn't wait for perfect conditions. They faced problems that could have stopped them, but instead they used those challenges to build purpose.

- **Martin Luther King** Jr. faced the problem of racial segregation and injustice in America. Instead of responding with hate or violence, he used peaceful marches, speeches, and community action to push for civil rights.

- **Malala Yousafzai** lived in a place where girls were banned from going to school. After being attacked for speaking out, she turned her personal tragedy into a global movement for education rights.

- **Greta Thunberg** saw leaders ignoring the urgent problem of climate change. Starting with a one-person school strike, she transformed her concern into a worldwide youth movement demanding action.

They all had one thing in common: they turned **problems into purpose.**

Step 1: Define the Real Problem

Most people struggle with solving problems not because they aren't smart, but because they don't fully understand the issue. It's like a doctor giving the wrong diagnosis. You can't fix what you haven't figured out.
A strong problem statement should be:

Clear
Use simple and direct language.

Specific
Describe exactly what's wrong, not a vague feeling or complaint.

Convincing
Explain why it matters.

Relevant
Connect it to the people or situation involved.

Measurable
Be able to track whether it improves—even if it's not a number.

Ask yourself:

1. **What is happening?** Be factual and objective.
2. **Why does it matter?** Explain the impact on you, others, or your goals.

Weak example: "Nobody cares at school."
Strong example: "In the past month, three students in our class have said they feel invisible during group work, and no teacher has addressed it. This lowers motivation and creates tension." Clear language leads to better solutions.

Step 2: Get to the Root Cause

Sometimes we fix a problem only for it to come back. Why? Because we treat the symptoms, not the source. Strong leaders ask, "Why is this happening?"

Five Whys Technique: Keep asking "why" 5 times related to the problem in hand.

Example:

1. Why are we always late with group projects? Because people turn things in late.
2. Why? They forget deadlines.
3. Why? Because no one clearly communicates.
4. Why? Because we don't set roles early.
5. Why? Because we skip planning meetings.

Now you know the real issue is poor planning, not laziness.

Fishbone Diagram: Another way to find causes. You list potential causes under categories, where each category is a full Full Five Why Technique.

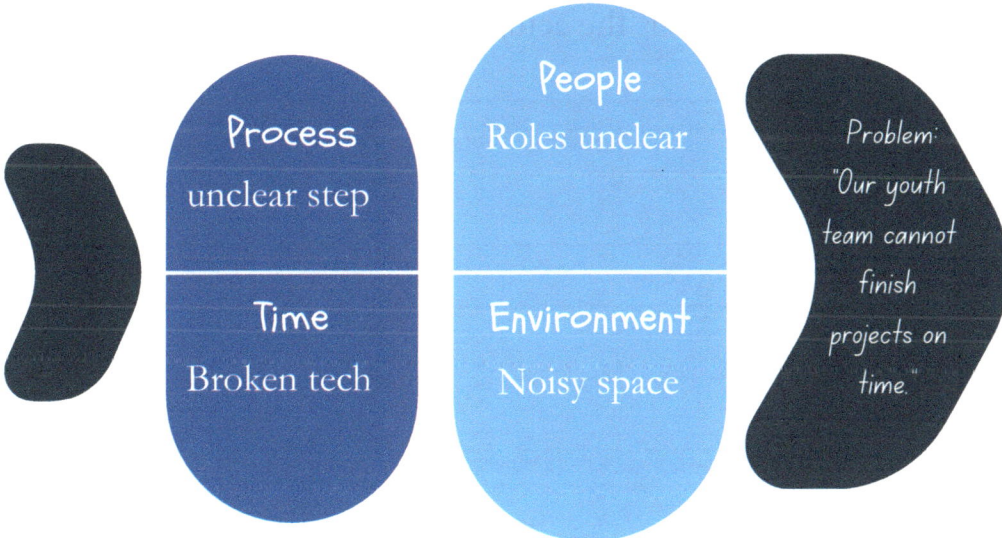

Seeing patterns helps you find real solutions. More on this in a few pages.

Whys Exercise

Instructions: Pick a problem and ask "Why?" five times in a row to explore the root cause. Write down each layer.

Problem:
_____

1. Why?
_____

2. Why?
_____

3. Why?
_____

4. Why?
_____

5. Why?
_____

Reflection: What is the actual root cause?
_____
_____
_____
_____
_____

Fishbone Diagram: What's Really Causing the Problem?

Instructions: Sometimes problems have more than one cause. A fishbone diagram helps you break a complex issue into smaller pieces.

Step 1: Write your main problem at the "head" of the fish (on the right).

Step 2: Choose 3–6 categories that might be contributing to the problem:

- People (e.g., miscommunication, lack of leadership)
- Environment (e.g., noisy space, distractions)
- Materials (e.g., broken tools, missing supplies)
- Process (e.g., unclear steps, skipped planning)
- Time (e.g., rushed decisions, procrastination)

Step 3: List specific causes as "bones" connecting to each category.

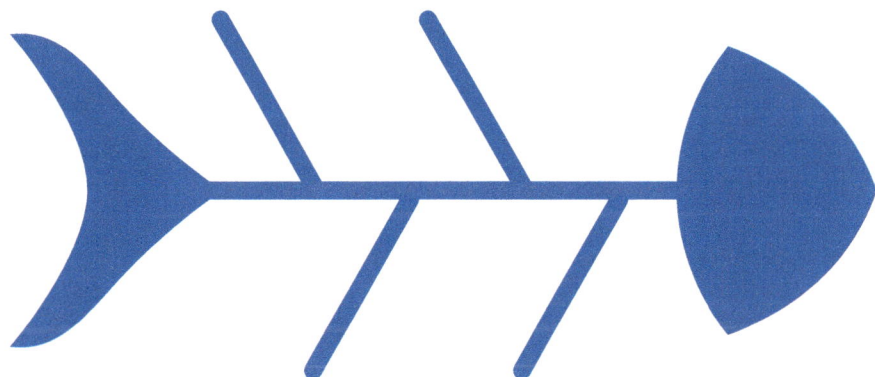

Example: Problem: "Our youth team cannot finish projects on time."

Category	Possible Cause:
People	Not everyone understands their role
Environment	Meetings are loud and disorganized
Process	No clear deadlines or reminders
Time	Other school commitments and distractions

ACTIVITY 4.3

REFLECTION TIME

After completing the diagram, ask yourself: Which category has the biggest impact, and where should we focus first?

_____

_____

_____

_____

Step 3: Focus Your Scope

Trying to fix everything at once leads to burnout. Instead, ask:

- What part of the problem can I realistically change?
- What's the most urgent or important piece?
- What does success look like?

Example:

- Big problem: "Teens feel overwhelmed."
- Focus: "Students struggle with deadlines."
- Success: "Start a peer study group that meets twice a week."

Zoom In – Scope Your Focus

Instructions: Pick a broad issue and narrow it down to something you can actually work on.

- **Broad Problem**: _____
- **Smaller, Solvable Part**: _____
- **What success would look like**: _____

Example:
- **Broad problem:** Students are stressed.
- **Focus:** Many struggle with deadlines.
- **Success**: Create a digital calendar for assignment tracking and share it with classmates.

ACTIVITY 4.4

Step 4: Make a SMART Plan

Don't just talk—plan. Use the SMART goal method:

- **Specific**: What exactly do you want to accomplish?
- **Measurable**: Can you track your progress?
- **Achievable**: Is it realistic with your time and skills?
- **Relevant**: Does it matter to you and your community?
- **Time-bound**: When will it be done?

Example: "I'll lead a team to create a digital planner and launch it at school within three weeks."

That's how leaders think.

SMART Goal Builder

Instructions: Use the SMART format to create a plan for solving a problem you care about.

S.M.A.R.T. Goal Component	What It Means
Specific	What do you want to do?
Measurable	How will you track progress?
Achievable	Is it realistic for your time and skills?
Relevant	Why does it matter to you or your community?
Time-bound	When will it be done?

Your Plan:

_____

_____

_____

_____

ACTIVITY 4.5

Step 5: Build a Strong Team

Great leaders don't go solo. They build teams. They:

- Listen.
- Communicate clearly.
- Trust and respect each other.
- Share responsibility.
- Create safe spaces for growth.

Teamwork equals trust in action. Don't lead with power. Lead with respect.

Step 6: Take Action, Then Reflect

The best part of problem solving? Doing something. It's not about perfection, it's about progress. Start small:

- Talk to someone.
- Write a plan.
- Try an experiment.
- Start a conversation.

Afterward, ask:

- What worked?
- What didn't?
- What did I learn about the problem and about myself?

Reflection turns every experience—success or failure—into growth.

Reflect and Grow

Instructions: Think about a project you've worked on recently. It could be any effort where you tried to solve a problem, help others, or make something better in school, your family, or your community.

Answer the following questions based on that project:

What was the problem you were trying to solve?

What steps did you take?

What part of your plan worked well?

What part could have been improved?

What did you learn about yourself as a problem solver?

If you could do it again, what would you do differently?

_____

_____

_____

_____

ACTIVITY 4.6

ACTIVITY 4.6 CONTINUED

Final Word

Leaders are made by solving problems. You don't have to be the loudest person in the room. You just have to care enough to take the first step. Even a small action—taken with heart—can spark real change.

REFLECTION TIME

- What's one problem in my life I've been treating like an obstacle instead of a real issue?

- How do I usually react to problems: avoid them, complain about them, or try to solve them?

- What do I learn about myself when I solve a problem, even a small one?

THINK ABOUT IT

1. You keep arguing with a sibling every morning. What's the real problem, and how would you solve it?

   _____
   _____
   _____

2. Your class keeps missing project deadlines. What problem-solving step could help your team get back on track?

   _____
   _____
   _____

3. A friend says, "Nobody listens to me." How would you help them define and solve the real problem?

   _____
   _____
   _____

5

Patience, Perseverance & Steadfastness

What Does "Strong" Really Mean?

When someone says "be strong," what comes to mind? You might picture someone lifting weights, standing tall in a crowd, or staying silent when they're angry. That's what the world often shows us—physical strength, toughness, being unbothered. But what if strength looks different?

- What if strength is staying kind when someone hurts you?
- What if it's finishing something even when you feel like quitting?
- What if it's holding your tongue when you really want to clap back?

That kind of strength isn't loud, but it's powerful. It's called **patience**. And it's one of the greatest strengths a leader can have.

Patience holds you steady when life gets shaky. It helps you breathe before reacting. It helps you grow when things feel slow or stuck. It's not about never feeling upset or stressed. It's about choosing to keep going—even when you feel like giving up.

So next time you want to quit, ask yourself: "What would a mountain do?"
A mountain doesn't run. It doesn't hide. It stands firm. And so can you.

Trigger Tracker – When I Want to Quit

Instructions: List three situations that test your patience. Then, write down your automatic reaction and a new response you want to practice.

Trigger (What tests my patience?)	My automatic reaction	My new response

Response ideas:

Take deep breaths. Step away and come back later. Count to ten.

ACTIVITY 5.1

Three Ways to Practice Patience

Patience isn't just sitting quietly and waiting. It's an active strength you use in different situations:

1. **Doing the Right Thing, Even When It's Hard**

Examples:

- Waking up early for practice when your bed is warm.
- Keeping up with your goals, even when you're tired.
- Being kind when you're annoyed.

2. Saying No to the Wrong Thing

Examples:

- Not replying to drama with more drama.
- Holding back a harsh comment.
- Saying no when someone pressures you to do something you know is wrong.

3. Staying Strong in Tough Times

Examples:

- Coping with a loss or disappointment.
- Getting a bad result after working hard and deciding to try again.
- Feeling lonely or overlooked but not letting it stop you.

You won't get it perfect every time. But every day gives you a chance to grow in one of these ways.

Some days, you need the strength to act. Other days, you need the strength to walk away. Sometimes you just need the strength to stay standing. That's what makes you mountain strong.

Why Patience Is Like a Mountain

Being mountain strong doesn't mean you never get tired or sad. It means you don't crumble when life is hard. A mountain:

- **Stands firm** in all kinds of weather.
- **Grows slowly,** but powerfully.
- **Lifts others,** giving support.

LEADERSHIP IN ACTION

Two friends both wanted new shoes. Sam didn't like working, so he kept asking his family for money and sometimes even took cash without permission. He never paid anyone back and wasted what little he got. When it came time to buy shoes, he had nothing.

Meanwhile, Keith decided to hustle the honest way. He mowed lawns, helped neighbors carry groceries, and saved a little each week. By the end, he had more than enough for the shoes. But instead of buying the flashiest pair, he chose a cheaper one and saved the rest. Keith realized that money earned through patience and hard work felt better than anything handed to him.

Grit Over Quick Wins

Anyone can look good when life is easy. The real test of leadership and character is how you respond when things get hard. **Grit** is what keeps you going.

- You feel the struggle.
- You take a breath and keep moving.
- You keep climbing, even when it's tough.

Real strength doesn't come from ease. It comes from effort.

ACTIVITY 5.2

My Perseverance Contract

Instructions: Fill in the blanks and sign your own commitment to patience and perseverance.

I, _____, choose to become mountain strong.

I will not always feel motivated, but I will keep moving.

When I feel like giving up, I will remind myself of my purpose, my values, and my support network.

I will take care of my mind, my heart, and my body.

I will seek help when I need it.

I will not compare my journey to anyone else's.

My prayers, my small steps, and my effort all matter.

Signed: _____ Date: _____

Real People, Real Patience

Patience shows up in everyday people:

- Someone who keeps helping others even when they're struggling themselves.
- A student who fails a test but decides to study smarter, not give up.
- A friend who chooses forgiveness instead of holding a grudge.

They don't wait for things to be easy. They stay kind, focused, and strong. That's patience in action.

Building Patience in a Fast World

Let's be honest: being patient is hard. Your phone buzzes. People test your limits. Everything feels slow. Patience isn't something you're born with. It's something you build—like a muscle. Start with small exercises:

- Count to ten before you respond when you're upset.
- Put your phone away for fifteen minutes and just sit with your thoughts.
- Wait a few minutes to eat or drink, even when you're hungry.
- Take a deep breath before speaking when someone interrupts you.

These are like mini-workouts for your self-control. You won't get it right every time. The goal isn't perfection. The goal is progress. Stay steady. Keep climbing. Every step you take with patience is a step toward becoming who you're meant to be. You don't need to be loud to be strong. You don't need quick wins to grow. You just need to keep going. That's what it means to be mountain strong. That's what it means to lead with patience.

REFLECTION TIME

- What situations test my patience the most, and how do I usually react?

  _____
  _____

- When was the last time I showed perseverance, even when it was hard?

  _____
  _____

- How does practicing patience make me a stronger leader?

  _____
  _____

THINK ABOUT IT

1. You study for weeks but fail a test. Do you give up, or try again with a new approach?
   _____
   _____

2. Your team keeps losing games even though you're putting in effort. How do you show patience and leadership?
   _____
   _____

3. A friend keeps pushing your buttons, hoping you'll snap. What's the patient response?
   _____
   _____
   _____

6

Time Management
Smart Hustle

Why Time Is a Big Deal

Time is one of the most valuable gifts you will ever have. You can't save it for later or get more when you run out. You can lose money and earn it back. You can feel tired and recover with rest. But once a moment is gone, it's gone.

That's why managing time is really about managing your life. It's not just a schedule or a to-do list. It's about using your hours in a way that shows who you are, what you care about, and who you want to become.

Smart leaders don't just stay busy. They stay purposeful. They don't fill every minute. They fill the right minutes with meaning.

Why Time Matters

Time is how we:

- Build character
- Grow relationships
- Learn new skills
- Chase our goals

Everyone has the same 24 hours in a day. What separates leaders from everyone else is how they use those hours. Ask yourself: *What does my time say about what I care about?*

Time Audit – Where Does My Time Go?

Instructions: For one full weekday, track everything you do in 30-minute increments. Be honest and specific. Create a table like this:

Time Block	What I Did	Was it Productive? (Yes/No)	Notes or Reflection
7:00 – 7:30 AM	Scrolled on phone in bed	No	Felt sluggish afterward
7:30 – 8:00 AM	Breakfast & morning prep	Yes	Helped start my day with calm & focus

ACTIVITY 6.1

ACTIVITY 6.1 CONTINUED

Time Block	What I Did	Was it Productive? (Yes/No)	Notes or Reflection

> **Reflect:**
> - How much of your time was used with intention?
> - What surprised you?
> - Where can you reclaim wasted time?
>
> _____
> _____
> _____
> _____
> _____

ACTIVITY 6.1 CONTINUED

Connect Your Time to Your Purpose

Without a sense of purpose, your calendar can fill up with things that don't matter. With purpose, even small tasks feel meaningful. Your purpose is the bigger mission behind your daily actions. It helps you decide what to say yes to, what to walk away from, and where to spend your energy. The clearer your purpose is, the better you'll be at protecting your time from distractions.

Priorities: Not Everything Deserves Your Time

Trying to do everything at once is a trap. Not every activity is worth your time. Before you say yes, ask yourself:

- Does this support my purpose?
- Does this help me grow?
- Would I still do this if no one praised me for it?

If the answer is no, it might not be a priority.

> ## LEADERSHIP IN ACTION
>
> Caleb wanted to start a small clothing business. He spent hours scrolling TikTok for "inspiration" but never worked on his designs. One day he tracked his time and realized he wasted almost 4 hours a day on his phone. Once he cut that in half, he finally launched his online shop. His success didn't come from working more—it came from using time with purpose.

Plan Your Time Like a Leader

You don't have to control every second, but you do need a plan. **Time Blocking** divides your day into blocks for specific tasks. For example:

- **Morning Block (6–9 AM):** Wake up, breakfast, morning prep
- **Day Block (9 AM–4 PM):** School or work, focus tasks
- **Evening Block (4–7 PM):** Exercise, family time, chores
- **Night Block (7–10 PM):** Homework, journaling, wind-down

Anchor Habits are small routines that keep you grounded:

- Checking your planner every morning
- Reflecting on your goals every weekend
- Preparing your bag and clothes each night

Protect Your Time

Time is fragile. You have to protect it from:

- **Distractions** – social media, endless scrolling, constant notifications
- **Procrastination** – fear or avoidance that delays important work
- **Overcommitment** – saying yes to too much and spreading yourself too thin
- **Lack of rest** – exhaustion that ruins even the best plans

Ask yourself:

- What are my biggest time-wasters?
- What small change can I make this week to use my time better?

The Power Hour – Start Your Day With Purpose

- Get out of bed without hitting snooze Eat a nourishing breakfast without your phone
- Read, reflect, or journal your goals for the day
- Go for a walk, stretch, or do a quick workout
- Start on your most important task before school or work
- Spend time in quiet reflection

Instructions: Pick **three mornings** this week to wake up a little earlier and commit to a "Power Hour." This is the first hour of your day spent with intention, not rushing. In your Power Hour, do one or more of the following:

Track your experience (on a piece of paper or your journal):

Day	What I Did in My Power Hour	How I Felt Afterward
1		
2		
3		

ACTIVITY 6.2

REFLECTION TIME

- Did starting early change how you felt or acted for the rest of the day?

  _____
  _____
  _____

- What's one thing you want to keep from your Power Hour routine?

  _____
  _____
  _____

- Did this help you start your day with more control, calm, and/or confidence?

  _____
  _____
  _____

Boost Your Time with Simple Tools

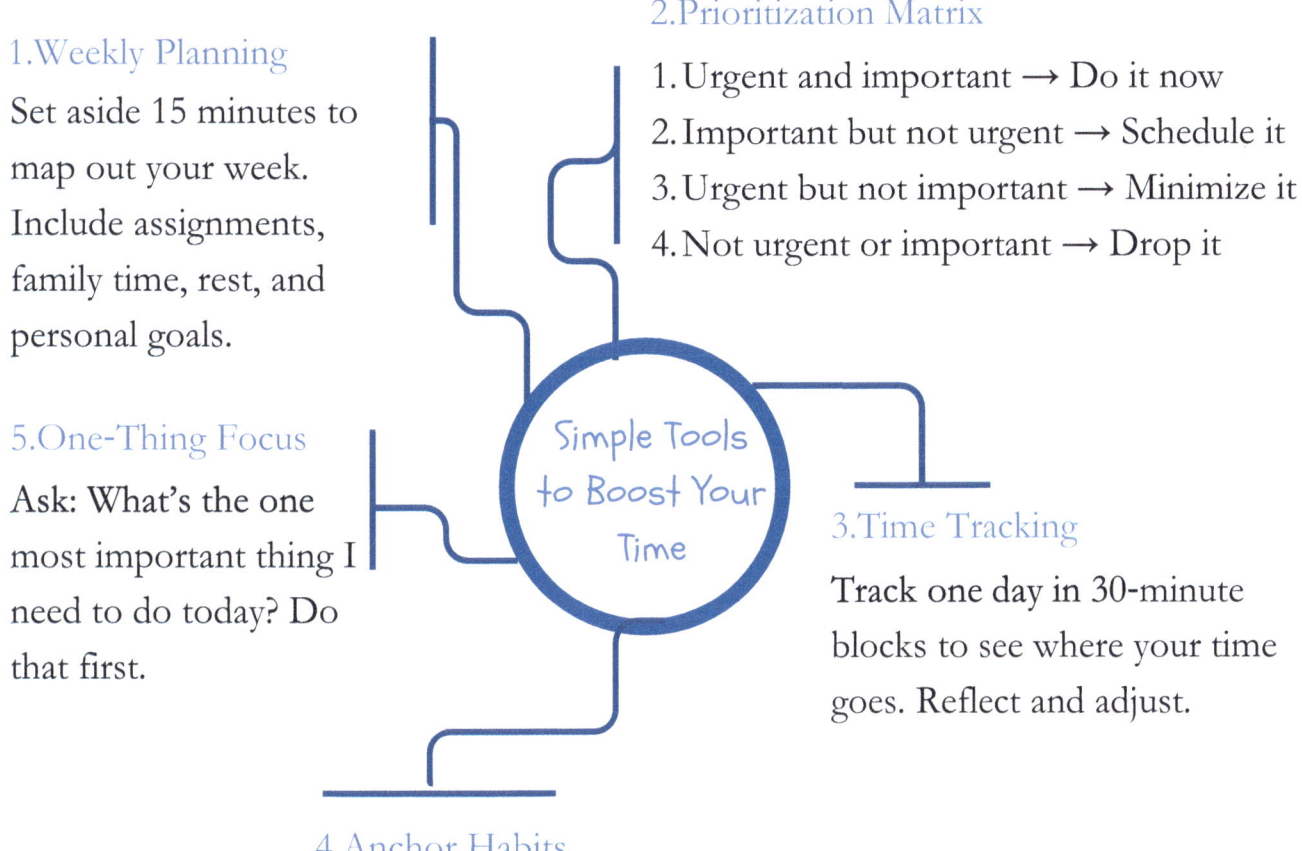

1. Weekly Planning
Set aside 15 minutes to map out your week. Include assignments, family time, rest, and personal goals.

2. Prioritization Matrix
1. Urgent and important → Do it now
2. Important but not urgent → Schedule it
3. Urgent but not important → Minimize it
4. Not urgent or important → Drop it

3. Time Tracking
Track one day in 30-minute blocks to see where your time goes. Reflect and adjust.

4. Anchor Habits
Attach habits to things you already do. For example:
- After breakfast → Review your planner
- Before bed → Reflect on your wins and lessons

5. One-Thing Focus
Ask: What's the one most important thing I need to do today? Do that first.

Balance Over Burnout

You're not a robot. You need to rest, recharge, and reset. Smart hustle includes balance:

- Balance between work and rest
- Balance between helping others and caring for yourself
- Balance between planning and staying flexible

Leaders protect their energy so they can lead for the long haul.

ACTIVITY 6.3

Balance Check – The 5-Part Wheel

Instructions: Draw a circle and divide it into five sections:

1. Learning and School
2. Personal Growth
3. Relationships
4. Health and Rest
5. Service or Hobbies

Rate how you focused on each area this past week, from 1 (low) to 10 (high). Shade each section like a wheel chart.

REFLECTION TIME

- Which areas are thriving? Which areas need more attention?
  _____
  _____
  _____

- What would help you find a better balance next week?
  _____
  _____

Design Your Weekly Plan

Instructions: Use a **digital planner,** calendar app, or printed weekly template to map out the upcoming week.

Don't just list tasks—plan for balance, growth, and rest.

Include these key areas:

- **Study Time:** Assignments, projects, and focused study blocks
- **Family and Relationships:** Time to connect with loved ones or help at home
- **Rest and Recharge:** Sleep goals, breaks, hobbies, or screen-free time
- **Personal Growth:** Reading, journaling, volunteering, or learning something new
- **Daily Goals:** One clear goal each day tied to your values or mission

Bonus Challenge:

Add one daily anchor habit—**a small, repeatable action that grounds you.**

Examples:

- Write a gratitude list after breakfast
- Review your goals after school
- Spend three minutes reflecting before bed
- Take ten minutes of quiet time or reading to start your day
- Do a stretch or breathing exercise before homework

ACTIVITY 6.4

Time Block	Mon.	Tues.	Wed.	Thurs.	Fri.	Sat.	Sun.
5:00–6:00 AM							
6:00–7:00 AM							
7:00–8:00 AM							
9:00–10:00 AM							
8:00–9:00 AM							
10:00–11:00 AM							
11:00–12:00 PM							
12:00–1:00 PM							
1:00–2:00 PM							
3:00–4:00 PM							
2:00–3:00 PM							
4:00–5:00 PM							
5:00–6:00 PM							
6:00–7:00 PM							
7:00–8:00 PM							
8:00–9:00 PM							
9:00–10:00 PM							

Weekly Planning Is Leadership in Action

Weekly planning helps you:

- Align with your purpose
- Avoid chaos and stress
- Build habits that last

A strong weekly plan includes:

- **Personal priorities** – things you care about most
- **School goals** – assignments and study time
- **Family and social time** – connecting with people who matter
- **Rest and recovery** – sleep and downtime

Start small. Stay consistent. Let your schedule reflect who you want to become. Time management isn't about doing more. It's about doing what matters. Every minute you use with intention builds your future. Hustle smart, protect your time, and lead your life.

REFLECTION TIME

- What's one time-waster I can cut back this week?

  _____
  _____

- How can connecting my time to my purpose help me feel less stressed?

  _____
  _____

- When do I feel most in control of my time, and why?

  _____
  _____

THINK ABOUT IT

1. You spend all week playing games and forget a big project. How do you reset your schedule?

_____

_____

2. A friend keeps texting during your study time. Do you ignore it, set a boundary, or give in?

_____

_____

3. You want more family time but also need to study. How can you balance both without burning out?

_____

_____

_____

Submission
Learning to Let Go and Lean In

Why Submission Matters

When people hear the word submission, they sometimes think it means weakness, giving up, or letting others walk all over you. But that's not what we mean here. Submission is about **accepting what's bigger than you and working with it instead of fighting it**. It's about recognizing that you can't control everything—and that's okay.

Think of it like water. When water meets a rock, it doesn't try to smash through. It flows around, over, and under. It bends without breaking. That's what leaders do when they practice submission: they know when to push, when to adjust, and when to trust the process.

Where Do You Push, Where Do You Flow?

Write down three situations in your life right now:

1. Something you can control.
2. Something you can partly control.
3. Something you can't control at all.

1. _____
2. _____
3. _____

Now ask yourself:

- What can I do about each one?
- What do I need to accept and let go of?

This is the balance of submission: action + acceptance.

_____
_____
_____
_____

ACTIVITY 7.1

Submission and Leadership

Strong leaders know when to **stand firm** and when to **submit to reality**.

- Your coach tells you to run laps even though you're tired. You submit to the training because it builds strength.
- Your parent sets boundaries you don't like. You submit to some rules because you know they care about your safety.
- Life throws pain your way. You submit to the fact you can't erase it—but you can choose how to respond.

Submission is not giving up. It's choosing to work with life instead of wasting all your energy fighting what you can't change.

LEADERSHIP IN ACTION

Meet David. He hated every rule in the facility. At first, he fought everything: the schedule, the guards, even the food line. He got in trouble daily.

One day, a mentor asked him, "What are you really fighting?" David realized he couldn't change the rules. What he could change was his response. Slowly, he submitted—not to give up, but to work smarter. He focused on what he could control: finishing schoolwork, reading, and staying out of fights.

By the end of the program, David said: "When I stopped fighting everything, things finally started working out." That's submission.

Strength Builder Submission

Think of one area in your life where you keep resisting, even though you can't fully control it. Maybe it's a rule, a routine, or a situation. Write:

- What would happen if I kept resisting?
- What might happen if I submit, accept, and focus on my response?

Compare your answers. Which path looks stronger?

_____
_____
_____

ACTIVITY 7.2

- When have I mistaken submission for weakness?

_____
_____
_____

- How does letting go of control in some areas actually make me stronger?

_____
_____

- Who do I respect that practices healthy submission, and what can I learn from them?

_____
_____

REFLECTION TIME

THINK ABOUT IT

1. Your teacher changes the assignment last minute. You feel frustrated. What's the submission move here?

___

___

___

2. A family member keeps setting boundaries you don't like. How do you balance respect with your own voice?

___

___

___

3. Your team loses a game even though you gave it your best. How can submission help you bounce back instead of quitting?

___

___

___

8

Purification
Clearing the Junk So You Can Lead

Why Purification Matters

Think about your phone. Over time, junk files, useless apps, and too many pictures slow it down. Eventually, you have to clear things out so it can run fast again. Life works the same way. We carry around dirt, stress, and bad habits that weigh us down. Purification is about **clearing the junk—inside and out —so you can move with confidence and lead with clarity.**

A leader who takes care of their body, mind, and choices earns trust. Nobody wants to follow someone who's messy, dishonest, or full of anger.

Physical Purification: Taking Care of Your Body

How you carry yourself matters. If you stay clean, eat well, and rest enough, you show others you respect yourself. Leaders don't have to be perfect, but they should set the tone.

- Brushing your teeth before class.
- Showering regularly.
- Keeping your clothes neat.
- Sleeping instead of scrolling all night.

These little habits add up. A clean, energized leader gives off strength.

Clean Start

Write down one small habit you can add this week to take better care of your body. Maybe it's drinking more water, sleeping an extra hour, or organizing your space. Try it for 7 days straight.

_____
_____
_____

ACTIVITY 8.1

Emotional Purification: Clearing Out Negative Stuff

We all carry junk inside—anger, jealousy, grudges, arrogance. If you don't deal with it, it spills out in your actions. A leader who's always mad or jealous loses respect fast.

Purification means checking yourself:

- Am I letting hate eat me up?
- Am I acting like I'm better than others?
- Am I holding grudges that make me bitter?

Letting go doesn't make you weak. It makes you lighter.

Trash Out

Think of **one negative feeling** that's been slowing you down. Write it on a piece of paper. Crumple it up. Throw it in the trash. Then write down one positive habit to replace it (like gratitude, patience, or kindness).

_____
_____
_____

ACTIVITY 8.2

Ethical Purification: Keeping It Real in What You Do

Purification isn't just personal. It shows in how you act towards others. A leader who cheats, lies, or steals can't be trusted.

Ask yourself:

- Do I handle money honestly?
- Do I own up when I mess up?
- Do I give back instead of just taking?

ACTIVITY 8.3

Scenario Check

Leaders with clean hands and clear choices inspire people. They don't just talk—they show what honesty looks like.

Read these quick scenarios. Circle which choice demonstrates pure leadership:

1. You borrow a hoodie and forget to return it. Do you
    (a) keep it or
    (b) give it back?
2. You find $5 on the floor. Do you
    (a) pocket it or
    (b) turn it in?
3. Your group project teammate slacks. Do you
    (a) lie for them or
    (b) tell the truth respectfully?

LEADERSHIP IN ACTION

Marcus had a reputation for being disorganized. He also fought with his classmates, made fun of people, and even lied to get out of trouble. One day, a friend told him straight up, *"You're not fun to hang out with anymore."* That hit him hard. For the first time, he realized how his habits were pushing people away.

So Marcus started small. He cleaned up his space, and stopped cracking mean jokes. He forced himself to be honest, even when it was uncomfortable. Over time, his friends noticed the difference. The same friend who once avoided him said, *"You're different now—you actually feel good to be around."* Marcus learned that when you clear out the junk—inside and out—people begin to trust and respect you again. That's purification in action.

My Purification Action Plan

Make a simple 3-step plan:

1. One physical habit I will work on:

_____

2. One emotional habit I will work on:

_____

3. One ethical habit I will work on:

_____

Keep it realistic. Start small.

ACTIVITY 8.4

REFLECTION TIME

- What "junk" in my life makes me feel heavy?

  _____
  _____

- How does cleaning up my body, emotions, or choices help me as a leader?

  _____
  _____

- Who in my life sets a good example of purification, and why?

  _____
  _____

THINK ABOUT IT

1. You're angry at a friend and keep replaying the argument in your head. What's the purification move here?

   _____
   _____

2. You skipped cleaning your space for a week, and now it's a mess. How do you reset?

   _____
   _____

3. A teammate cheats in a game and wants you to cover for them. Do you protect them or purify the moment by being honest?

   _____
   _____

9

Communication
Say It Clear, Say It Real

Why Communication Matters

Have you ever had a fight with a friend just because of a text message that came out wrong? Or gotten in trouble because you didn't tell someone what was really going on? That's the power of communication. It can **build trust or break trust**. Good leaders know how to speak clearly, listen well, and share information before problems explode. Think about it: teams win when they talk. Families work better when people share. Even in tough places like school or lockup, the ones who communicate respectfully usually earn more respect back.

Basics of Clear Communication

Communication isn't just talking. It's how you talk.

Introduce yourself with confidence.
A simple "Hi, I'm Jordan" can open doors.

Make requests with respect.
People respond better when you show you value them.

Ask for help politely.
Instead of "Yo, I need this now," try "Can you help me figure this out?"

First Impressions

Pair up with someone. Pretend you're meeting a teacher, coach, or mentor for the first time. Practice introducing yourself. Notice how tone, eye contact, and posture change the vibe.

_____
_____
_____
_____

ACTIVITY 9.1

Giving Updates & Being Proactive

Here's a leadership truth: **don't wait until the last minute to speak up**. If you're stuck on a project, let people know early. If you're behind, update your team. Silence makes small problems grow into big ones.

The Stuck Student

Imagine you've been struggling on homework for two days and it's due tomorrow. What would you say to your teacher? Write down your message. Keep it clear, honest, and respectful.

_____
_____
_____
_____

ACTIVITY 9.2

Asking for Feedback the Right Way

Feedback isn't an attack—it's a tool. Leaders ask for feedback because they want to grow. Instead of saying: "What do you think?"

Try: "Can you check if my explanation makes sense?"
The more specific you are, the better the help you get.

ACTIVITY 9.3

Feedback Request

Write a short sentence asking for feedback on something real in your life (a drawing, a project, a goal). Practice saying it out loud to a peer.

_____
_____
_____

Do's and Don'ts of Communication

Do	VS	Don't:
Be clear.		Be vague.
Respect people's time.		Ignore messages or emails.
Say thank you.		Get defensive when someone gives feedback.

Leaders own their words—and they make them count.

Message Makeover

Take this text: *"idk… maybe I'll do it, whatever."* Rewrite it into a strong, clear message that shows responsibility.

_____

_____

_____

_____

ACTIVITY 9.4

LEADERSHIP IN ACTION

Ayman was assigned group work. He got sick and fell behind on his assigned part. He didn't tell anyone he was behind. The night before the deadline, the whole team found out. They failed the project—not because Ayman didn't care, but because he didn't ask for help and his team members did not reach out. Later, Ayman said: *"If I had just spoken up earlier, we could've fixed it."* Good communication could have saved the day.

REFLECTION TIME

- When was a time I misunderstood someone because they weren't clear?

- What makes me nervous about asking for help?

- How can I use feedback to grow instead of taking it personal?

THINK ABOUT IT

1. You're assigned a task in class but don't understand it. Do you stay quiet or speak up? What's the better move?

2. A friend texts you in an angry tone, but you're not sure if they meant it that way. How do you handle it?

3. You're leading a group and notice someone slacking. How do you communicate without starting drama?

10

Communication with Adults Make the Click, Bridge the Gap

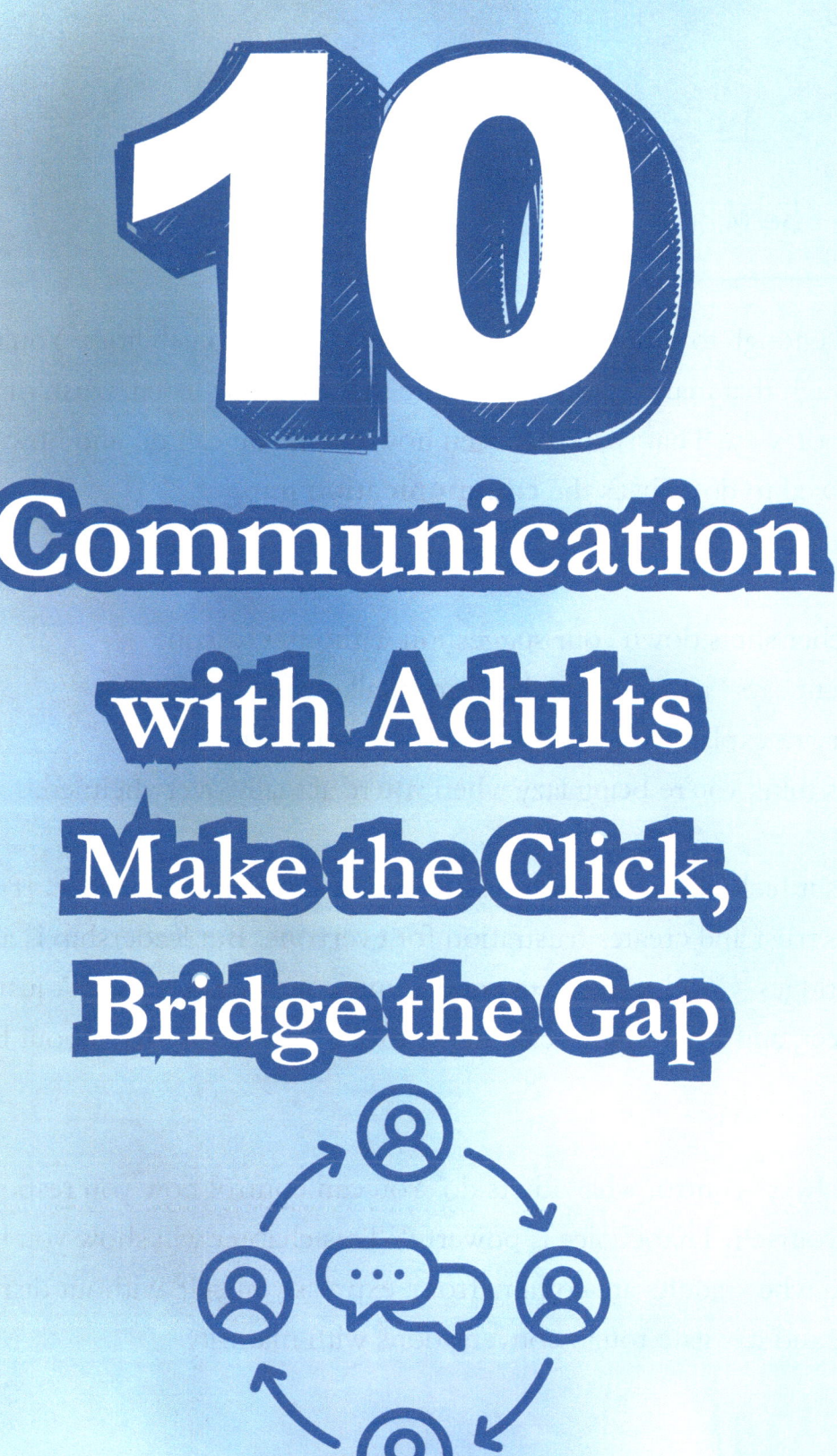

You're in the Middle

You're old enough to think deeply and take on real responsibilities. You're still young enough that many adults in your life may not fully listen, trust, or understand your point of view. That space between how much you can do and how much you're allowed to do? That's the **communication gap.**
You might see it when:

- A teacher shuts down your suggestion without a reason.
- A parent says "because I said so" and walks away.
- You try to explain yourself, but an adult hears "attitude."
- Adults think you're being lazy when you're actually overwhelmed.

Sometimes it feels like a wall. Sometimes it feels like a broken bridge. If you ignore it, it blocks trust and creates frustration for everyone. But leadership is about building bridges. Good leaders are good communicators. They don't just talk; they listen, reflect, and adjust. They care more about connection than about being "right."

You can't always control what adults do. You can control how you respond and how you carry yourself. That choice is powerful. This chapter will show you how to understand where adults are coming from, express yourself without disrespect, listen well, and navigate tough conversations with maturity.

Communication Iceberg

Instructions: Draw an iceberg that's half above the water and half below. Label the top part "What They Say" and the bottom part "What Might Be Underneath."

Example:

- What They Say: "You're always on your phone."
- What Might Be Underneath: "I feel like we're growing distant."

ACTIVITY 10.1

REFLECTION TIME

Think about a common comment from an adult that frustrates you. What might be underneath it?
Write a short paragraph about how understanding the "beneath" could change your reaction.

_____

_____

_____

Why Miscommunication Happens

Miscommunication isn't random. It usually happens when something important is missing:

Lack of clarity

You might say, "I need space," but an adult hears, "I don't care." They might give advice, but you hear it as control. The problem isn't always what is said; it's how it's heard.

Assumptions and mistrust

You might assume they don't get it. They might assume you're being rude. When you both guess what the other person thinks, it blocks real connection.

Different goals

You want independence. They want safety. Neither of you is wrong; you're just aiming at different things.

Generational and cultural gaps

Adults grew up in a different world with different rules and pressures. What feels normal to you might feel strange to them. What feels respectful to them might not make sense to you.

When you recognize these patterns, you can start to change them.

The Art of Communication

Communication is about connection—not just expressing yourself. Good communication means:

- Being clear and calm
- Speaking with intention
- Listening without interrupting
- Choosing the right tone

Words carry weight. They can build relationships or break them. You don't need to talk the most; you need to talk with purpose. Listening is a superpower. Real listening earns trust and shows maturity. You don't always have to agree, but you do have to try to understand.

Seeing from Their Side

You might feel like adults don't get it. Maybe they don't, but trying to understand their side helps you communicate better.

- **They're human too**
  Adults have fears, past experiences, and stress. They make mistakes. Seeing them as people—not just authority figures—can shift how you respond.

- **They might be trying to protect you**
  Even when it doesn't show perfectly, strictness often comes from care. Many adults truly want what's best for you.

- **They grew up differently**
  Technology, mental health awareness, and communication styles have all changed. Some adults are learning as they go.

Understanding their perspective doesn't mean you have to agree. It helps you choose the best way to approach conversations.

Speaking Up with Strength

Talking well is a skill. You don't have to be loud; you have to be thoughtful.

- **Tone matters**

    Saying, "You never listen" feels like an attack. Saying, "I don't feel heard, and it makes me frustrated" invites understanding.

- **Timing matters**

    Don't start serious conversations when someone is tired, hungry, or angry. Asking, "Is now a good time to talk?" shows respect.

- **Character matters**

    Speak with kindness, even when you're upset. That's strength.

- **Mistakes happen**

    If you lose your cool, own it. Say, "I'm sorry I said it like that. Here's what I meant." Fixing mistakes builds trust.

LEADERSHIP IN ACTION

James kept clashing with his mom. Every time she asked about homework, he snapped back, "I got it, stop nagging me." One day, instead of yelling, he asked, "Can I tell you why I get frustrated when you ask me like that?" His mom explained she worried he'd fall behind like his older cousin. James realized her "nagging" was really fear. That moment didn't fix everything, but it built trust. The wall started turning into a bridge.

Listening Like a Leader

Listening is more than staying quiet. It's about being present. Real listening means:

- Letting the other person finish
- Staying calm, even when you disagree
- Asking thoughtful questions
- Staying curious instead of defensive

You won't always agree with adults, but you can always try to understand. Listening shows respect and opens doors for better conversations.

Disagreeing with Respect

You don't have to stay silent when something feels wrong. But how you speak up matters.

- Use phrases like, "I see where you're coming from, but I'd like to offer another view," instead of, "That makes no sense."
- Decide if your goal is to be right or to be understood.
- If emotions are high, ask for a break. "Can we talk in a few minutes? I need to cool down." Taking space shows maturity.

You can disagree without disrespect. That's real strength.

Talk with Intention

Before a big conversation, pause and ask yourself:

- What's my goal?
- What's the best way to say this?
- Is now the right time?

Speak to connect, not just to react. Words are powerful. Use them to build bridges, not burn them. Not every conversation will go perfectly. Every respectful effort counts. Keep trying, keep learning, and keep leading.

ACTIVITY 10.2

Communication Style Check

Instructions: Put a ✓ next to the statements that sound like you:

- ☐ I raise my voice when I feel misunderstood.
- ☐ I avoid talking when things get tense.
- ☐ I try to stay calm, even when I disagree.
- ☐ I interrupt when I get excited or passionate.
- ☐ I listen until the other person is done before I speak.

Reflection:
Pick one strength and one weakness from your answers. What can you do to improve how you communicate?

_____
_____
_____

Pause Before You Speak

Instructions: Before a difficult conversation, take a quiet moment to ground yourself. You can:

- Take a few deep breaths.
- Set a clear intention ("I want to be calm, respectful, and honest")
- Say a personal affirmation ("I'm speaking to connect, not to win")

Then, fill in:

- One adult I want to improve communication with:

  _____

- *One conversation I want to have with them:*

  _____

- *One goal I want from this conversation:*

  _____

Bonus: Role-play this conversation with a friend, mentor, or family member. Practice using a calm tone and respectful language.

ACTIVITY 10.3

Respectful Comebacks

Instructions: *Match each tense phrase with a respectful comeback:*

Tense Phrase	Respectful Comeback
"You are being so dramatic."	"I may not know everything, but I want to learn from you too."
"This is not up for debate."	"I want to try again. Can we both listen this time?"
"You never listen!"	"I understand you're upset. Can I ask a question to help me understand?""
"You are too young to get it."	"I feel strongly about this and want to explain why it matters to me."

Reflection: Come up with your own respectful comeback for a phrase you've heard at home or school.

_____
_____
_____
_____

ACTIVITY 10.4

REFLECTION TIME

- When was the last time I felt misunderstood by an adult? How did I react?

  _____
  _____

- What's one thing I can do to make adults feel like I'm listening more?

  _____
  _____

- Which is harder for me: speaking up respectfully, or staying calm while listening?

  _____
  _____

THINK ABOUT IT

1. A teacher shuts down your idea without hearing you out. How do you respond?

   _____
   _____

2. Your parent says "because I said so" and won't explain. How can you communicate without losing respect?

   _____
   _____

3. You disagree with a coach's rule during practice. How can you speak up without creating conflict?

   _____
   _____

11

Self-Awareness
Acing My Game

Catch Yourself in the Moment

Have you ever said something and immediately thought, "Why did I say that?" Or snapped at someone when you were actually just tired, not angry? That tiny moment when you realize what happened is a glimpse of self-awareness.

Self-awareness means understanding what's going on inside you—your feelings, your thoughts, and how they affect the way you act. Imagine having a mirror that reflects not just your face, but your heart and mind too. The clearer you see yourself, the more power you have to grow, lead, and make better choices.

Being self-aware doesn't mean you're perfect. It means you're honest with yourself and working to improve. You notice when you're stressed. You catch yourself before saying something hurtful. You understand why certain things make you happy or upset.

My Emotion Tracker

Instructions: Make a chart with columns for Time, Emotion, What triggered it, How I responded, and What I could do differently. Fill it out for three days (one or two entries per day).

Time	Emotion	What Triggered It	How I Responded	What I Could Do Differently
Morning				
Afternoon				
Evening				

ACTIVITY 11.1

REFLECTION TIME

Which emotion came up most often? What surprised you about your triggers or responses?

_____
_____
_____
_____
_____

Why Knowing Yourself Matters

Leadership isn't just about telling people what to do. It's about understanding people—including yourself. If you can't manage your own emotions, it becomes tough to manage a team, a classroom, or even a friendship. Many of the most effective leaders aren't just book smart; they're emotionally smart.

Experts call this "emotional intelligence." It's the ability to recognize and manage your own emotions and understand how others feel. Self-awareness is the foundation. Think of it like a video game: if you don't know your own stats—your power, weaknesses, energy levels—you won't get very far. Self-awareness helps you level up. You don't need to look far for examples. Think of athletes who keep their cool under pressure or activists who stay calm when others shout. They don't just react; they respond with thoughtfulness. That's emotional strength. That's leadership.

So, next time you feel a big emotion, pause and ask yourself:
- What am I feeling?
- What am I thinking?
- What can I do about it?

That short pause can make all the difference.

My Strengths and Growth Areas

Instructions: Create two columns: "Things I Do Well" and "Things I Want to Improve." Write three to five items in each. Think about school, family, friendships, and personal interests.

Things I Do Well	Things I Want to Improve

Reflection Prompt: How can your strengths help you grow in the areas you struggle with?

_____
_____
_____

ACTIVITY 11.2

LEADERSHIP IN ACTION

> Jose always snapped when teammates joked about him missing shots. He thought they were just being mean. One day, a coach pulled him aside and said, "Notice how angry you get the second someone teases you? That's not about them—it's about how you see yourself." Jose realized his trigger wasn't the jokes; it was his own fear of failing. Once he named it, he learned to laugh it off, focus on practice, and improve. His self-awareness didn't just change his attitude—it changed his game.

Your Inner Compass

Your feelings, thoughts, and actions are connected—like three parts of a triangle. When you understand each one, you can move with clarity instead of confusion.

Feelings – What's going on inside your heart?

Feelings are signals. You might feel nervous before a test, excited about a game, hurt by a friend's words, or peaceful during a quiet moment. Feelings aren't good or bad. They're just messages telling you something is happening. Problems arise when we ignore those signals or let them take over without understanding them.

Thoughts – What is your brain telling you?

Your brain is powerful. Sometimes it tells stories that aren't true: "No one likes me," "I'm going to fail," "I have to be perfect." Just because you think something doesn't mean it's true. Being self-aware means pausing to ask: "Is this thought helpful? Is it real? Or am I just tired, hungry, or stressed?"

> ### Actions – What do you do with all this?
>
> Your actions result from what you feel and think. If you're angry and think someone is against you, you might shout. But if you pause, notice your anger, and change your thought, you might decide to talk it out instead. Leaders don't just act; they respond with wisdom.

So when you find yourself in a big moment, use those three questions—what am I feeling, thinking, and what should I do—as your compass.

Your actions result from what you feel and think.

The Building Blocks of Emotional Intelligence

According to researchers, emotional intelligence includes five key parts:

1. **Self-awareness** – Knowing your feelings and what causes them.

2. **Self-regulation** – Managing your emotions so they don't control you.

3. **Motivation** – Staying driven even when things get tough.

4. **Empathy** – Understanding how others feel.

5. **Social skills** – Communicating clearly and working well with others.

Emotional intelligence helps you communicate better, handle stress, make smarter decisions, build stronger relationships, and become a trusted leader. It's not about being perfect. It's about practicing, reflecting, and growing.

Leadership Self-Check Quiz

Instructions: Rate yourself (1 = rarely, 5 = always) on statements like:

- I know what I'm feeling and why.

  Rating: _____

- I ask for help when I need it.

  Rating: _____

- I reflect on my behavior after an argument.

  Rating: _____

- I stay calm in tense moments.

  Rating: _____

- I welcome feedback from others.

  Rating: _____

Reflection Prompt:

Which area do you want to work on most? Who could help you improve it?

_____
_____
_____
_____

ACTIVITY 11.3

"Pause and Choose" Scenarios

Instructions: Here are three real-life situations:

- Your sibling takes your stuff without asking.
  Answer the following questions:

  What would you feel?

  _____
  _____
  _____

- What would you want to do?

  _____
  _____
  _____

- What you should do as a leader?

  _____
  _____
  _____

- You get a bad grade on something you studied hard for.
  Answer the following questions:

  What would you feel?

  _____
  _____
  _____

- What would you want to do?

  _____
  _____
  _____

ACTIVITY 11.4

ACTIVITY 11.4 CONTINUED

- What you should do as a leader?

  _____
  _____
  _____

- A friend cancels plans last minute, again. Answer the following questions:

  What would you feel?

  _____
  _____
  _____

- What would you want to do?

  _____
  _____
  _____

- What you should do as a leader?

  _____
  _____
  _____

  Reflection Prompt: What's one thing that helps you pause before reacting?

  _____
  _____
  _____

Your Leadership Superpower: Self-Awareness

The best leaders know themselves. They understand:

- Their strengths and how to use them.
- Their triggers and how to manage them.
- Their values and how to protect them.

Because they know themselves, they lead others with authenticity. Self-awareness helps you:

- Stay focused when things get stressful.
- Own your mistakes and learn from them.
- Pause before saying or doing something you might regret.
- Build relationships based on trust and understanding.

Great leaders aren't afraid to look inward. They know that real growth begins there. You can build that inner mirror too. Let's start acing the game—from the inside out.

My Daily Check-In Template

Instructions:

Create a 3-question daily check-in that you can use in a notebook or notes app:

1. What did I feel most strongly today?
2. What did I do well today?
3. What can I do better tomorrow?

Bonus Challenge: Try it for 7 days straight and share your biggest insight.

_____
_____
_____
_____

Self-awareness is your inner compass. The more you practice recognizing your feelings, thoughts, and actions, the better you'll navigate life's challenges. Use these tools to understand yourself, respond wisely, and build leadership from the inside out.

ACTIVITY 11.5

REFLECTION TIME

- What's one thing I learned about myself this week that surprised me?

  _____

  _____

- When do I feel most confident and when do I feel most insecure?

  _____

  _____

- How do I usually react to feedback—defensive, or open to growth?

  _____

THINK ABOUT IT

1. A teacher says you're distracted in class. You disagree. How do you respond with self-awareness?

   _____

   _____

2. A friend tells you you're being too controlling in a group project. How do you take that feedback?

   _____

   _____

3. You notice you always get angry when someone teases you. What's a self-aware way to handle it?

   _____

   _____

Anger Management
Turning Heat into Power

Why Anger Matters

Everybody gets angry. It's a normal human feeling. The problem isn't anger itself—it's what we do with it. Uncontrolled anger can wreck friendships, get you into fights, or make people afraid to trust you. But controlled anger? That's power. Leaders know how to feel the heat without letting it burn everything down. Think of fire. Fire can destroy a house. But fire can also cook food or keep you warm. Anger works the same way—it's dangerous if wild, but useful if controlled.

Step 1: Notice Your Anger

The first step in anger management is noticing when it shows up. Everyone has signals:

- Heart beating fast.
- Fists clenching.
- Face getting hot.
- Wanting to yell or break something.

Leaders pay attention to those signals so they can choose how to respond.

My Anger Signals

Write down at least three signs that show you're getting angry. Do you get quiet? Loud? Do you feel it in your body? Be honest—this is your personal anger map.

_____

_____

_____

_____

ACTIVITY 12.1

Step 2: Change Your Thoughts

Anger often grows from how we *think* about a situation. If you tell yourself "they disrespected me on purpose," your anger spikes. If you reframe it—"maybe they're having a bad day"—it cools down.

Changing your thoughts doesn't mean excusing bad behavior. It means giving yourself space to respond with strength instead of rage.

ACTIVITY 12.2

Reframe the Scene

Think of a time you got angry recently. Write down the thought that fueled your anger. Now write a calmer version of the same thought. Compare the difference in how you feel.

_____

_____

_____

_____

_____

Step 3: Healthy Outlets for Anger

Bottling up anger is as bad as exploding. Leaders find safe ways to let it out:

- Talking it out with someone you trust.
- Writing in a journal.
- Exercising.
- Taking a break.

Unhealthy outlets—like fighting, breaking stuff, or shutting down—only make things worse.

Two Columns

On one side of a page, list unhealthy ways you've dealt with anger. On the other side, list healthy ways you could deal with it. Circle one healthy optionto try next time you feel the heat.

ACTIVITY 12.3

LEADERSHIP IN ACTION

Tyler got mad when a teammate kept bumping into him during football practice. He snapped, cursed him out, and stormed off. The team stopped trusting him after that. Later, Tyler tried something new. He apologies to his teammate and the next time someone bumped into him, he paused, breathed, and said, "excuse me, I think you are too close, could you give me some space?" The team actually respected him more. He learned: controlling anger didn't make him weak—it made him stronger.

Step 4: Build Your Anger Plan

Every leader needs a personal plan. Ask yourself:

1. What are my top 3 triggers?

2. What are 2 strategies I'll use when I feel anger rising?

3. Who can I go to when I need to cool down?

Having a plan ready helps you act with control, not regret.

ACTIVITY 12.4

My Anger Plan

Write out your answers to the 3 questions above in your journal or a piece of paper. Keep it somewhere you can see it when you need a reminder.

_____
_____
_____
_____
_____

REFLECTION TIME

- When was the last time I lost my temper? How could I have handled it better?

  _____
  _____

- What signals show me I'm about to get angry?

  _____
  _____

- How can controlling my anger make me a stronger leader?

  _____
  _____

THINK ABOUT IT

1. A classmate keeps talking over you during group work. How do you handle it without blowing up?

   _____
   _____

2. A family member pushes your buttons on purpose. What's your move?

   _____
   _____

3. You feel anger rising during a game after someone cheats. Do you walk away or fight?

   _____
   _____

13

Risk analysis & Smart Choice

Fine Line Between Courage & Stupidity

Everyday Decisions

Every day you make choices. Some are small, like what to wear or when to start homework. Others feel big, like whether to stand up to a bully or how to respond when your friend dares you to do something risky. The choices you make shape who you become. Why do we make the choices we do? Many of our decisions are driven by feelings—wanting to fit in, avoiding pain, or seeking approval. These feelings are real, but they can cloud our judgment. Sometimes we think we're being brave when we're just reacting to pressure. Sometimes we think we're being careful when we're actually missing a chance to grow. Smart leadership begins when you pause and ask yourself, "Why am I making this choice?"

Risk Reflection Map

Instructions:

1. Think of a real situation where you took a risk (or avoided one).
2. Fill out the reflection chart below:

Situation	What did I do?	What was at risk?	What happened?	Would I do it again? Why or why not?

Sample Response:

Situation: I stood up for someone being bullied.

What I did: I told the group to stop and walked the person to class.

What was at risk: Being laughed at or targeted.

What happened: They backed off and left me alone.

Would I do it again: Yes. It was scary, but it was the right thing to do.

Courage vs. Impulse

Being a leader doesn't mean always saying yes or always saying no. It means thinking before you act. Courage isn't doing something risky just because it's scary. It's doing something important because it's right—even if it scares you.

Consider two teens:

- One jumps off a bridge on a dare because "everyone else is doing it."
- The other speaks up when they see someone being bullied, even though it might make them a target.

Both take risks. One is about pressure. The other is about principle. The decisions we make reveal who we are becoming. Are we reacting, or responding with purpose?

ACTIVITY 13.2

Courage or Careless?

Instructions: For each scenario below, write whether the person showed Courage or acted Carelessly. Then explain why.

Scenario 1: A student sneaks out after curfew to meet friends.

_____

_____

Scenario 2: A classmate reports cheating on a test, even though they might lose friends.

_____

_____

Scenario 3: Someone posts a video mocking a teacher to get more likes.

_____

_____

LEADERSHIP IN ACTION

Maya's friends dared her to skip class and hang at the mall. She almost said yes, but paused to think: What's my real goal? Her objectives were to stay on the basketball team, keep her grades up, and maintain her parents' trust.

She listed her options: go with them, say no, or suggest hanging out after school. The "fun" option risked detention and suspension from the team. The smarter option kept her on track and still gave her time with friends later. Maya chose to wait, and that one decision protected her goals and showed her friends what real courage looks like—thinking before acting.

What Makes a Smart Choice?

Smart choices are both brave and careful. They come from thinking, not just feeling. They consider both short-term and long-term consequences. A quick test:

- Impulsive choice: "It felt right in the moment."
- Smart choice: "I thought about my values, my options, and the consequences."

Smart leaders ask themselves:

1. What am I trying to accomplish?
2. What could go wrong if I act—or if I don't?
3. Does this match my values and goals?

Smart choices can look like:

- Walking away from a fight, even if others call it weak.
- Taking on a leadership role, even when it scares you.
- Saying no to a trend that doesn't align with your values.
- Speaking up respectfully, even when no one else does.

Smart decisions aren't always exciting. They earn trust, build character, and set you up for real success.

Steps to a Smart Decision

1 **Define the Problem**

Ask: What's actually going on? Why is this situation hard or important?

2 **Identify Your Objectives**

Ask: What are my goals here? Which values do I want to protect?

3 **List Your Alternatives**

Ask: What are three different ways I could respond to this situation?

4 **Consider the Consequences**

Ask: What are the risks and rewards of each option? Will I regret this later?

Smart choices come from clear thinking and strong values—not just feelings.

My SMART Decision Chart

Instructions: Choose a real or hypothetical decision you are facing. Use the chart to compare 2–3 options by scoring each on:

- Safety
- Meaning
- Accountability
- Respect
- Trust

Option	Safety	Meaning	Accountability	Respect	Trust	Total

Remember: the highest score isn't always "easiest." Write a short reflection about what your scores tell you.

Reflection:

_____

_____

_____

Activity 13.3

Pros & Cons Chart – What's the Real Choice?

Pick a risky decision you might face (joining in on a dare, standing up to a bully, skipping responsibilities). Make two columns: "Pros" and "Cons."

- Write down every possible upside and downside you can think of.
- Circle the one or two points that matter most.
- Do the pros outweigh the cons—or am I just chasing the short-term rush?

ACTIVITY 13.4

Set Strong Objectives

Objectives are your targets—the outcomes you care about. They guide your decisions. Let's say you're thinking about speaking up in a group that's being unfair. Your objectives might be:

- Be honest without hurting others.
- Promote fairness. Stay respectful.
- Protect your emotional well-being.

Break It Down with Sub-Objectives

Big goals can feel overwhelming. That's why strong leaders break them into smaller steps.

Main Objective:
"I want to resolve a disagreement with my teammate respectfully."

Sub-Objectives:

- Calm down before I respond.
- Listen openly to their side.
- Speak honestly without blaming them.

Small wins lead to big wins. Sub-objectives build momentum, confidence, and clarity.

Explore Your Options

You usually have more than one path forward. Smart leaders list and compare them. For example, suppose your friend wants you to skip school. Your options might be:

1. Go with them.

2. Say no and explain why.

3. Offer to hang out after school.

4. Talk to a trusted adult.

Then ask:

- Is this safe?
- Does it align with my values?
- Can I take responsibility for this decision?
- Will I be proud of it later?

If it helps, rate each option on a scale from 1 to 5 based on these questions. Compare the totals. Remember: the highest score isn't always the easiest, but it can guide you toward what matters most.

Build Your Personal Risk Wisdom Toolkit

Smart decision-making isn't just about moments. It's about habits. Build a system that supports you:

REFLECTION TIME

Step away from distractions before big choices. Think about what truly matters.

_____

_____

_____

THINK ABOUT IT

People respond better when you show you value them. Ask: Why am I doing this? Would I still do it if no one was watching? Would I want someone I care about to make this choice?

Trusted People List

Know 1–3 people you can turn to when you're unsure—mentors, teachers, or friends.

Top Values List

Write down your top five values (like honesty, courage, or kindness) and review them before making a decision.

Calm-Down Strategy

When emotions run high, pause. Breathe. Walk. Listen to music. Let your mind settle.

Decision Journal

After big choices, jot down what happened, what you learned, and what you might do.

My Risk Wisdom Toolkit

Create your own set of tools and habits to help you make smart, confident choices. Use the table below to brainstorm:

Tool / Habit	What it helps me do	How I will use it regularly
Self-check questions	Pause and reflect on why I'm making this choice	Keep a list in my phone to review before big decisions
Trusted people to talk to	Get honest feedback and support	Talk to a mentor, teacher, or friend when I feel unsure
Top 5 personal values	Stay aligned with what matters to me	Write them in my journal or keep them on my wall
Calm-down strategy	Reset when emotions are high	Take a walk, breathe deeply, or listen to music to relax
Weekly reflection	Learn from my experiences and decisions	Write 3 sentences each Sunday night

ACTIVITY 13.5

Final Thought

Taking risks is part of life. But not every risk is worth taking. Real strength is in the pause. Real wisdom is in patience. Real leadership is being able to say:

"This choice reflects my values. I made it thoughtfully, and I'm okay with the outcome."

If you can say that, you're already leading.

> **REFLECTION TIME**
>
> - What's the riskiest decision I've made lately, and how did it turn out?
>   _____
>   _____
>
> - Do I tend to act too quickly, or overthink until I freeze?
>   _____
>   _____
>
> - How can slowing down help me make smarter choices?
>   _____
>   _____

THINK ABOUT IT

1. Your friends dare you to jump off a roof into a pool. What's the smart move?

   _____

   _____

2. You want to defend a friend being picked on. How do you know if your action is brave or reckless?

   _____

   _____

   _____

3. You're offered a chance to make quick money in a sketchy way. How would you use smart choice tools before deciding?

   _____

   _____

   _____

14

Rights & Obligations

My World

Respect Is a Two-Way Street

Everyone is born with basic rights like life, dignity, safety, and freedom of thought. These aren't things you earn; they belong to you simply because you're human.

But here's the truth: with every right comes a responsibility. If you want respect, you also have to give it. If you want safety, you shouldn't harm others.

Leaders understand this balance. They don't just focus on themselves, but they stand up for the rights of others too. They practice fairness, compassion, and justice in their families, schools, and communities.

ACTIVITY 14.1

Rights & Responsibilities Match

Instructions: Draw lines to connect which responsibilities go with which rights.

Rights	Responsibilities
Respect	Helping
Safety	Listening
Voice	Honesty
Learning	Not harming others

Reflection Prompt: What happens if people only claim rights without living up to responsibilities?

_____

_____

Respecting Everyone's Rights

Every person is owed certain basic rights just for being human. These include:

- Life: the right to live safely without violence or harm.
- Dignity: the right to be treated with respect and not humiliated or devalued.
- Ownership: the right to keep what belongs to you and not have it taken away.
- Freedom of Thought : the right to think, believe, and express your ideas.

We need to protect these rights because without them, trust, safety, and fairness collapse. If people can be disrespected, silenced, or hurt without consequence, no community can thrive. Protecting rights makes sure everyone has the chance to grow, belong, and contribute.

Strong leaders recognize that rights aren't just about themselves. It's not leadership to demand your own dignity while ignoring someone else's. Leadership means making sure others' rights are respected, too.

When leaders protect rights, they build justice, trust, and respect, and people are more willing to follow someone who stands for everyone, not just themselves.

ACTIVITY 14.2

Everyday Rights Check

Instructions: Write down 3 times this week when you saw someone's rights respected, and 3 times when someone's rights were ignored.

Rights Respected:

1. _____
2. _____
3. _____

Rights Ignored:

1. _____
2. _____
3. _____

Reflection Prompt: How did those moments change the way people felt or acted?

_____
_____
_____

Balancing Rights with Responsibilities

Rights don't stand alone. They come with responsibilities. If you want your rights respected, you also need to live up to the obligations that come with them.

Think about the different roles you hold:

- In your family: You have the right to be cared for, but you also have the responsibility to help out, show respect, and be honest.

- At school: You have the right to learn, but you also have the responsibility to do your work, listen, and not block others from learning.

- In your community: You have the right to safety and belonging, but you also responsibility to follow rules, respect others, and give back when you can.

Leaders know how to balance the two. They don't just demand their rights while ignoring their responsibilities. They model fairness by holding themselves accountable.

When people see you living up to your obligations, they're more likely to trust you when you speak up about your rights. That balance is what makes leadership steady and respected.

My Role, My Responsibility

Instructions: In three columns, write one right and one responsibility you have in your family, school, and community.

Role	My Right	My Responsibility
Family	_____	_____
School	_____	_____
Community	_____	_____

Reflection Prompt: How does balancing rights with responsibilities build trust?

_____
_____
_____

ACTIVITY 14.3

> ## LEADERSHIP IN ACTION
>
> At the local recreation center, some teens always grabbed the best equipment and left a mess for everyone else. It caused arguments and made the space feel unfair.
>
> A small group decided to step up. They reminded others to share, helped clean up, and made sure everyone got a turn. Before long, the vibe shifted. The recreation center felt more respectful and welcoming.
>
> Their leadership showed that protecting rights and taking responsibility isn't just personal, it strengthens the whole community.

Empathy: Seeing Beyond Yourself When people's rights aren't respected, real harm happens. It can be:

- Physical: being hurt, unsafe, or neglected.
- Emotional: feeling disrespected, ignored, or belittled.
- Social: being excluded, stereotyped, or treated unfairly.

Leaders don't just notice harm after it happens. Instead, they try to prevent it. That's where empathy comes in.

Empathy means imagining how someone else feels and caring enough to act. When you put yourself in another person's shoes, you start to see the weight of their struggles. And you're less likely to cause harm yourself.

Empathy makes leaders stronger. It helps them respond with patience instead of anger, fairness instead of bias, and support instead of silence.

A leader who practices empathy builds trust because people know they won't just look out for themselves, but they'll look out for others too.

Step Into Their Shoes

Instructions: Think of a time when someone's rights weren't respected. Write how you would feel if it happened to you. Then write one empathetic action a leader could take to make it better.

What happened:
_____
_____
_____

How it would feel:
_____
_____
_____

What a leader could do:
_____
_____
_____

Reflection Prompt: How does empathy help prevent harm?
_____
_____
_____

ACTIVITY 14.4

Being a Good Citizen

Leaders understand that respecting rights and fulfilling obligations isn't only personal, it's also social. Good citizenship means more than just following rules. It's about actively contributing to your community.

Being a good citizen looks like:

- Respecting laws so everyone can live in safety and order.
- Serving your community, whether that's volunteering, helping a neighbor, or supporting a cause.
- Standing up for justice, even when it's uncomfortable, by speaking against prejudice, bullying, or unfair treatment.

Leadership and citizenship go hand in hand. When you act as a good citizen, you show others what it means to live with integrity.

People trust leaders who don't just talk about rights and responsibilities but practice them daily.

Citizenship is leadership in action since it proves you're committed to something bigger than yourself.

My Citizenship Plan

Instructions: Write down 2 ways you can respect rules or laws, 2 ways you can serve your community, and 1 way you can stand up for justice.

Respect rules/laws:

1. _____

2. _____

Serve my community:

1. _____

2. _____

Stand up for justice:

1. _____

Reflection Prompt: How do these actions show leadership?

_____

_____

_____

ACTIVITY 14.5

REFLECTION TIME

- Why is it important to balance rights and responsibilities?

- How does empathy make you a stronger leader?

- What's one right you can stand up for in your family, school, or community?

THINK ABOUT IT

1. Your teacher blames you for something you didn't do. What's a fair and respectful way to respond?

2. Two friends are fighting because one always takes what they want without asking. How would you handle it as a leader?

3. You see a classmate being excluded from a group activity. What could you do to practice empathy and fairness?

15

Wealth & Patience
Building Without Breaking

What Wealth Really Means

When people say "wealth," most think of money. But wealth is bigger than cash. It's also your time, health, skills, relationships, and opportunities. A rich life isn't just about dollars—it's about how you use what you've got.

Patience is the secret ingredient. Without patience, people blow their money fast, waste their chances, or ruin relationships. With patience, you can grow wealth slowly, steadily, and wisely.

Wealth Beyond Money

Imagine you wake up with:
- A healthy body.
- A safe place to stay.
- People who care about you.
- Skills you can grow.

That's wealth. Leaders learn to see the value in what they already have, not just what's in their pockets.

My Wealth List

Write down five things you have right now that make you "wealthy" besides money. Example: "I can draw well," "I'm good at math," "I have a cousin who's always got my back."

_____
_____
_____
_____
_____

ACTIVITY 15.1

Patience With Money & Choices

Impatience with money leads to bad moves: spending fast, gambling, or chasing quick fixes. Patience means planning, saving, and waiting for the right time. Think about someone who spends their whole check in a day. Compare them to someone who saves a little each week. A month later, who's in better shape?

$100 Challenge

If you were given $100 today, what would you do? Spend it all? Save part of it? Use some to learn a new skill? Give some away? Write your choice and explain how patience plays a role in your decision.

_____
_____
_____
_____

ACTIVITY 15.2

Investment Beyond Cash

Leaders invest in more than money:

- **Skills:** Learning is an investment in yourself.
- **Time:** Using time wisely pays off later.
- **Relationships:** Treat people well, and it comes back around.
- **Giving:** Sharing what you have makes your community stronger.

These "investments" take patience. You don't see results overnight—but they grow.

ACTIVITY 15.3

Wealth Builder Plan

Pick one area (skills, time, relationships, or giving). Write one thing you can do this week to invest in it. Example: "Practice basketball for 20 minutes a day," "Help my sibling with homework," "Save $5."

_____

_____

_____

_____

LEADERSHIP IN ACTION

Lamar always wanted fast money. He borrowed, spent, and showed off. Soon, he was broke, stressed, and in debt.

James, on the other hand, was patient. He worked small jobs, saved up, learned a trade, and gave back a little to others. Over time, James built trust, skills, and real stability. Both started with little. Patience made the difference.

REFLECTION TIME

- What does wealth mean to me, beyond money?
  _____
  _____

- When have I been impatient with money or resources?
  _____
  _____

- How can I practice patience with wealth in my daily life?
  _____
  _____

THINK ABOUT IT

1. You get your first paycheck and want to buy shoes right away. What's the patient move?
   _____
   _____

2. A friend pressures you to gamble or spend money fast. How do you respond?
   _____
   _____

3. You're saving for something big, but it feels slow. What can keep you motivated?
   _____
   _____

16

Fairness

Playing It Straight

Why Fairness Matters

Nobody likes being treated unfairly. Maybe a teacher blamed you for something you didn't do. Or maybe your sibling got the bigger slice of pizza when it was meant to be shared. Unfairness stings—it breaks trust fast.

Fairness means treating people with honesty and balance, not letting anger, favoritism, or bias decide your actions. For leaders, fairness is the backbone of respect. Without it, people stop following.

What Does It Mean to Be Fair?

Being fair isn't always about making everyone happy. It's about making sure rules and choices are applied equally.

- Listening to all sides before deciding.
- Not playing favorites.
- Using facts, not feelings, to judge.
- Owning up if you make a mistake.

My Fair & Unfair Moments

Write down one time you felt treated fairly. Then write one time you felt treated unfairly. How did each situation make you feel?

_____
_____
_____
_____

ACTIVITY 16.1

Why Should We Be Fair?

Fairness keeps peace. When people feel they're treated equally, they trust you more. Unfairness creates resentment and fights.

Think of a referee in a game. If the ref calls fouls fairly, players respect the game. If the ref is biased, players lose trust and the game falls apart. Leadership works the same way.

As a leader, people are watching how you handle decisions—big and small. If you're fair, even those who don't get their way will respect the process, because they know you listened and weighed things honestly. But if you play favorites or act on impulse, people stop believing in you. Fairness shows consistency, and consistency builds trust.

When trust grows, so does teamwork. People are more willing to follow your lead, share ideas, and give their best effort because they know they'll be treated with honesty. That's why fairness isn't just about avoiding drama. Fairness is the foundation that makes leadership strong and lasting.

How to Practice Fairness

Being fair doesn't mean every decision is easy. In fact, fair choices are often the hardest ones, because they might upset people you care about. But leaders who practice fairness earn long-term respect, even if not everyone is happy in the moment.

Here are some ways to practice fairness every day:

Check your bias.
Don't decide after listening to only one side of the story. Fairness means giving people a chance to speak.

Hear everyone out before acting
Ask yourself: Am I favoring a friend over someone else? Am I being harder on one person just because I don't like them?

Admit mistakes
Nobody is perfect. If you realize later that you made an unfair call, owning up and correcting it shows real leadership.

Be consistent.
If a rule applies to one person, it should apply to everyone. If you let one teammate slack off, but punish another for the same thing, people lose trust.

Stay calm
Anger clouds judgment. Taking a pause before deciding helps you think about what's truly fair.

Fairness takes practice, but every fair choice builds your reputation. When people know you'll treat them with balance and honesty, they'll trust you even in tough situations.

Role-Play

Pretend you're a team leader dividing up chores or tasks. Practice giving everyone a fair share without favoritism. Afterward, talk about how it felt.

_____

_____

_____

_____

_____

ACTIVITY 16.2

LEADERSHIP IN ACTION

Coach Davis always started the same five players, no matter how hard the others worked in practice. After a while, the bench players stopped giving their best—why bother if they'd never get a chance? The team's energy dropped, and even the starters grew frustrated.

One day, Coach Davis decided to change. He began rewarding effort, not just talent. Players who showed hustle and teamwork in practice earned playing time. The shift wasn't easy, but it made a difference. The team played with more heart, because they knew the coach's decisions were fair. Fairness didn't mean everyone got the same treatment, but it meant everyone had a real chance to earn their spot.

ACTIVITY 16.3

My Fairness Pledge

Write down one way you'll practice fairness this week. Maybe it's sharing equally, listening before judging, or stopping yourself from favoritism.

_____
_____
_____
_____
_____

REFLECTION TIME

- When did I feel treated unfairly, and how did it affect me?

_____
_____

- What makes it hard for me to be fair sometimes?

_____
_____

- How can fairness make me a better leader?

_____
_____

THINK ABOUT IT

1. Two friends want you on their side during an argument. How do you stay fair?

　

　

2. You're leading a group project, and your best friend isn't pulling their weight. Do you give them a pass or hold them to the same standard?

　

　

3. You see someone get punished harder than others for the same mistake. How could fairness be applied?

17
Resume Writing
Telling Your Story on Paper

Why Resumes Matter

Imagine you're trying to get a job, but the employer knows nothing about you. How do you show them you're the right person? That's where a resume comes in. A resume is like your personal highlight reel. It's not your whole life story, but it's the quick, clear version of your skills, experiences, and strengths. Employers use it to decide who to call in for interviews.

Even if you've never had a job before, you still have experiences worth sharing—school projects, sports, volunteering, or helping out in your community.

What Goes Into a Resume

A strong resume usually has:

- **Contact Info** (your name, phone, email).
- **Education** (where you go to school, grades if strong).
- **Skills** (things you're good at—teamwork, writing, fixing tech, organizing).
- **Experience** (any jobs, chores, community work, group projects).
- **Achievements** (awards, leadership roles, accomplishments).

Resume Inventory Sheet

- Babysitting your cousin.
- Running errands for the family.
- Playing on a team.
- Helping with a school event
- Learning to code, draw, or cook.

_____
_____
_____
_____
_____
_____

ACTIVITY 17.1

Don't judge it yet—just list it all. You'll sort later.

Tailoring Your Resume

Not every job is the same. If you're applying to work in a store, highlight teamwork and customer service. If you're applying for yard work, highlight responsibility and hard work.

Think of your resume like a playlist—you rearrange songs depending on the mood. Tailoring your resume means showing the skills that fit the job best.

Activity 17.2

Match the Job

Pick a role you'd like to apply for (cashier, camp counselor, tutor, etc.). Circle the items on your inventory that match that role. Write a sentence or two showing how those experiences prepare you.

_____
_____
_____
_____

Common Mistakes to Avoid

- Spelling errors.
- Making it too long (keep it one page).
- Being vague ("worked with people") instead of specific ("helped five classmates with homework").
- Lying (employers can spot it).

Leaders show honesty—even on paper.

Resume Do-Over

Sometimes we write about our experiences in a way that's too vague. Employers want details. A weak sentence is like a blurry picture; a strong sentence is clear and sharp.

Step 1: See the Example

Weak sentence: *"Did stuff at school."*

Strong sentence: *"Helped organize a school fundraiser that raised $200."*

Notice how the strong sentence shows **what** you did and **the result**.

Step 2: Practice Together

Rewrite these vague lines into stronger ones:

- *"Helped in class."*

  _____

  _____

- *"Worked at home."*

  _____

  _____

- *"Played sports."*

  _____

  _____

(Hint: Add details like numbers, results, or responsibilities.)

Step 3: Apply It to Your Life

Pick one vague experience from your Resume Inventory. Rewrite it into a strong, clear sentence you could put on your resume.

_____

_____

ACTIVITY 17.3

LEADERSHIP IN ACTION

Brianna wanted to apply at a local coffee shop but thought, "I don't have any job experience." When her mentor asked her to make a list of everything she'd done, she realized she had more to offer than she thought: school projects, babysitting, running track, volunteering at her church.

She tailored her resume for the coffee shop, highlighting teamwork from track, responsibility from babysitting, and communication skills from volunteering. The manager told her later that her resume stood out because it showed action and results, not just tasks.

Turns out, Brianna had plenty to offer—she just needed to put it on paper.

ACTIVITY 17.4

Build Your First Resume Draft

Using your inventory, create a short one-page draft. Even if it's rough, it's a start. Ask a peer or mentor to look it over and suggest one way to make it stronger.

Reflection Time

- What did I learn about myself while building my resume?
  _____
  _____

- What skills do I have that I didn't realize were valuable before?
  _____
  _____

- How can I keep improving my resume over time?
  _____
  _____

THINK ABOUT IT

1. You're applying for a job, but all you have is volunteer work. How do you show it's valuable?

___

2. A friend tells you to "just make stuff up" on your resume. How do you respond?

___

3. You're nervous your resume looks empty. What's one step you can take to strengthen it right now?

___

18

Job Hunting

Finding Your First Opportunity

Why Job Hunting Matters

Writing a resume is like sharpening your arrow before hunting. But a bow and arrow are useless if you never aim for a target. Job hunting is the part where you go out and actually **find opportunities**.

Many teens think, "Nobody will hire me, I don't have experience." But here's the secret: everyone starts somewhere. Employers aren't just looking for years of work —they're looking for **attitude, effort, and reliability.**

Where to Look for Jobs

Job opportunities aren't just posted on fancy websites. You can find them in everyday places:

- **Local businesses:** corner stores, fast food, grocery stores, barbershops, and community centers.
- **Schools:** tutoring, helping teachers, sports scorekeeping.
- **Community & faith centers:** volunteering that can lead to part-time roles.
- **Online**: websites and apps (Indeed, Snagajob, etc.) for entry-level postings.

My Job Map

Even if you can't go out right now, you can still think about where jobs exist.

Step 1 (Inside): Write down 2–3 jobs that exist right here in your environment (for example: kitchen, cleaning, tutoring, library).

Step 2 (Future): Write down 3–5 places in your home community where you could realistically ask about jobs once you're out (like shops, gyms, rec centers, restaurants).

_____

_____

_____

_____

_____

ACTIVITY 18.1

How to Approach Employers

Walking into a store and saying "Are you hiring?" might feel scary. But confidence goes a long way. Tips:

- Dress neat (even if casual).
- Be polite: "Hi, I'm [name]. Are you looking for help right now or soon?"
- Bring a copy of your resume.
- Thank them, even if they say no.

ACTIVITY 18.2

Role-Play

Practice with a partner. One person plays the "store manager," the other plays the job seeker. Switch roles. Practice introducing yourself and asking about openings.

Using Your Network

Sometimes the best jobs don't get posted—they get passed along through people you know. That's called networking.

- Tell friends and family you're looking for work.
- Ask teachers, coaches, or mentors if they know opportunities.
- Don't be shy—most people are glad to help.

ACTIVITY 18.3

My Network List

Write down five people you could ask for job leads (family, teachers, neighbors, mentors). Circle one person you'll reach out to this week.

_____
_____
_____
_____
_____

Staying Patient in the Hunt

Job hunting takes patience. You might hear "no" a lot before you get a "yes." That doesn't mean you're a failure. It means you're learning resilience.
Remember: every "no" brings you closer to the right "yes."

LEADERSHIP IN ACTION

Taylor wanted a job but didn't have experience. Instead of waiting, she started helping out at her community center—setting up chairs, passing out flyers, tutoring younger kids. She treated it like a real job: showing up on time and being dependable.

After a month, the director offered her a paid role helping run weekend events. Taylor realized that sometimes the door to a job isn't a job posting—it's showing up, serving, and proving you can be trusted.

REFLECTION TIME

- Where in my community can I realistically find job opportunities?
_____
_____

- Who can I ask to help me in my job search?
_____
_____

- How do I handle rejection without giving up?
_____
_____

19

Learning Never Stop Growing

Sometimes the best lessons are hidden. Did you miss a bus because you didn't check the schedule?

That's a lesson in planning. Did you babysit younger cousins and realize how much patience it takes?
That's a lesson in responsibility.

Leaders see both the obvious and hidden lessons. They don't shrug off mistakes or random moments. They ask, "What did I just learn from this?" That habit turns daily life into a classroom.

Hidden Lessons

Think about a time outside of school when you learned something important. Write it down. How did that lesson help you in real life?

_____

_____

_____

_____

ACTIVITY 19.1

Fixed vs. Growth Mindset

Your mindset is the way you see your own abilities. **A fixed mindset says:** *"This is just who I am. I'm either good at it or I'm not."* With this mindset, failure feels like proof that you're not capable. **A growth mindset says:** *"I might not get it yet, but I can improve if I keep working and learning."* With this mindset, failure isn't the end, it's feedback.

Leaders choose the growth mindset because it builds humility and openness. It takes humility to admit, "I don't know this yet." And it takes openness to keep trying when things are tough. That attitude shapes how you respond to challenges: do you shut down, or do you push forward and adapt?

The good news is that a growth mindset can be developed. Start by adding one word: "yet." Instead of saying, "I can't do this," say, "I can't do this yet." Then back it up with action: ask questions, practice more, and remind yourself that every skill takes time. Over time, this mindset makes you more resilient and stronger as a leader.

ACTIVITY 19.2

Mindset Check

Write down one challenge you faced. Underneath, write how a fixed mindset would see it, and how a growth mindset would see it.

_____

_____

_____

_____

_____

_____

Active Participation

Just showing up isn't enough. You can sit in a classroom, a team meeting, or a workshop and still learn nothing if you're tuned out. Leaders understand that just being present doesn't equal growth.

Being engaged by listening closely, asking questions, and practicing what you learn makes the difference. When you're engaged, the same hour that might have been wasted becomes an hour of real progress. You remember more, understand deeper, and gain skills you can actually use.

When you give your full attention, you show that what's being shared matters and that you're serious about growing. As a leader, that attitude sets the tone for others.

That's how active participation not only helps you learn, but it also raises the energy and focus of the whole group.

Listening Practice

Pair up. One person talks for one minute about something they enjoy. The other person's job is to listen without interrupting—then repeat back what they heard. Switch roles.

_____

_____

_____

ACTIVITY 19.3

Learning Tools: Notes & Questions

Good learners don't just let information pass through their ears. They capture it, think about it, and ask questions to make it stick.

Notes Matter.

Documenting what you learn is like creating your own personal playbook. Notes help you remember details later, but they also show what stood out to you. Instead of trying to write every word, focus on:

- Key ideas or steps.
- Examples you can use again.
- Action items you want to try.

At your level, even a simple method works:

- Use bullet points.
- Highlight or star the most important parts.
- Add a quick reflection at the end, like: "This reminds me of…" or "Next time I'll try…"

Questions Drive Growth

Great questions don't just get quick answers. They open the door to understanding. Learning-driven questions go beyond "yes/no." They start with why, how, or what if.

- Instead of: "Is this on the test?"
- Try: "Why does this work that way?" or "How can I use this outside of class?"

Leaders ask questions not just to get information, but to connect what they're learning to real life. That curiosity turns knowledge into power.

Strong Questions

Write down one "clarifying" question (to make sure you understand) and one "deep" question (to push for more insight) about a topic you've studied or something from this book.

_____
_____
_____
_____
_____

ACTIVITY 19.4

Turning Learning Into Action

Knowledge without action is like carrying around tools you never use. It doesn't help anyone. You can learn about time management, communication, or teamwork all day, but if you never practice those skills, nothing changes.

Leaders know that learning isn't complete until it's applied. Taking what you've learned and putting it into action builds confidence and shows others you're serious. For example:

- You learn about managing your time, try using a planner or setting reminders.
- If you learn about patience, practice it the next time someone tests you.
- If you learn a new skill at work or school, use it on your next project.

The moment you apply knowledge, it turns into growth. And when others see you taking action on what you've learned, they start to trust your leadership. Leaders don't just collect lessons, they also live them.

ACTIVITY 19.5

Learning-to-Action Plan

Write down one thing you've learned recently. Next to it, write one way you'll actually apply it this week.

_____
_____
_____
_____

LEADERSHIP IN ACTION

Sofia struggled in math and used to tell herself, "I'm just bad at this." One day, her teacher challenged her to change that thinking: "You're not bad at it, but you just haven't learned it yet."

Instead of giving up, Sofia tried a new approach. She started asking more questions in class, taking short notes to remind herself of the steps, and practicing a little each day. Slowly, her confidence grew.

When she finally solved a tough problem on her own, she realized that learning wasn't about being perfect right away. It was about being open, patient, and willing to keep trying.

REFLECTION TIME

- What's one unexpected place I've learned something valuable?
  _____
  _____
  _____

- How can a growth mindset help me face challenges?
  _____
  _____
  _____

- How can I turn what I've learned into action this week?
  _____
  _____
  _____

THINK ABOUT IT

1. You keep failing at a new skill. Do you give up or keep practicing with a growth mindset?

_____

_____

2. A teacher is explaining something, but you zone out. What's a better move?

_____

_____

3. You learn something useful from a peer. How do you show respect and use that lesson?

_____

_____

20

Basics of Thinking

Sharpening Your Mind

Why Thinking Matters

Everybody thinks, but not everybody thinks well. Sometimes we react without thinking and regret it later. Other times, we pause, reflect, and make a smarter choice. The difference is control. Reacting is automatic do it without realizing, often based on emotion. Thinking is intentional. You stop, consider options, and choose. Leaders know the difference because thinking gives them control over their choices. A leader who thinks before acting is less likely to blow up, make unfair decisions, or miss opportunities. Thinking is more than just knowing facts. It's about **how you use your mind** to solve problems, make decisions, and create new ideas.

Quick Decisions vs. Careful Thinking

Not all choices need deep thought. Some decisions like what snack to eat or what song to play are low-stakes. Quick reactions are fine there. But other decisions like how to respond when someone disrespects you, or whether to join in on a risky dare require careful thinking.

Leaders know when to react fast and when to slow down. They recognize that careful thinking protects them from mistakes and gives them the power to choose wisely.

React vs. Reflect

Write down two examples from your life:

- A time you reacted fast without thinking. What happened?

_____

_____

- A time you slowed down and thought carefully. How did that change the outcome?

_____

_____

ACTIVITY 20.1

What Good Thinking Needs

Good thinking doesn't just happen—it takes practice. Strong leaders build habits that make their thinking clear and reliable. Here's what it takes:

- Focus — Paying attention to the problem instead of getting distracted by emotions, rumors, or what everyone else is doing. Leaders zoom in on the real issue.
- Curiosity — Asking "why?" and "what if?" instead of settling for the first answer. Curiosity helps leaders see hidden options and opportunities.
- Fairness — Considering all sides, not just your own. A fair thinker doesn't make decisions based only on personal bias or anger—they look at the bigger picture.
- Evidence — Basing choices on facts, not just feelings. Leaders who use evidence earn trust because their decisions arc grounded in reality.

When leaders think with focus, curiosity, fairness, and evidence, people trust them more. They're less likely to jump to conclusions or make reckless choices. Instead, they show consistency, balance, and wisdom which is the kind of thinking that others want to follow.

ACTIVITY 20.2

Debate Both Sides

Pick a simple question: Should schools require uniforms? Write one reason for and one reason against. Notice how seeing both sides sharpens your thinking.

Reason for:

_____

_____

Reason against:

_____

_____

Types of Thinking

There's more than one way to think, and strong leaders know how to use the right type of thinking at the right time.

- **Analytical Thinking:** Breaking a problem into parts and looking at details. Leaders use this when they need to solve practical challenges, like planning a schedule or figuring out why a team isn't meeting deadlines.

- **Creative Thinking:** Generating new ideas and seeing possibilities others might miss. Leaders use creativity when brainstorming fresh solutions, coming up with new projects, or motivating people in fun ways.

- **Critical Thinking:** Asking tough questions and testing if something makes sense. Leaders use it to spot flaws in a plan, fact-check information, or avoid falling for bad advice.

- **Reflective Thinking:** Looking back on past actions to learn from them. Leaders use reflection to improve after mistakes, celebrate wins, and prepare better for the future.

Leaders rarely use just one type of thinking. For example, solving a team conflict might start with analytical thinking (what exactly happened), need creative thinking (how can we fix it differently this time), require critical thinking (does this solution really work), and end with reflective thinking (what did I learn for next time).

The best leaders combine these modes of thinking depending on the situation like tools in a toolbox.

Thinking Sampler

Try these quick challenges:

- Solve a riddle (analytical).

    I have keys but no locks. I have space but no room.
    You can enter but can't go outside. What am I?

    _____
    _____

- Imagine a new product teens would love (creative).

    _____
    _____

- Read a headline and ask, "Is this true? How do I know?" (critical).

    _____
    _____

- Write about one choice you made last week and what you'd do differently (reflective).

    _____
    _____

ACTIVITY 20.3

Innovative Thinking: Asking the Right Questions

Smart solutions don't come from guessing or rushing. They come from asking the right questions. Leaders don't stop at the surface answer. They dig deeper until they understand the real problem. One tool is **root-cause analysis:** keep asking "why" until you uncover what's really going on.

For example, why am I always late? Because I oversleep. Why do I oversleep? Because I scroll on my phone too long. The real problem isn't being late, it's not managing bedtime. When you know the root cause, you can fix the problem for good.

Another tool is **brainstorming:** writing down as many ideas as possible without judging them at first. Creative ideas often sound weird at the beginning, but they can spark the perfect solution once you refine them.

Strong leaders use both approaches. They dig deep with questions to find the real issue, then brainstorm to create new ways forward.

Innovative thinking isn't magic. It's the discipline of asking better questions and exploring better answers.

Five Whys

Pick a common problem you face (like being late, missing homework, or fighting with a sibling). Ask "why" five times and see where it leads.

_____

_____

_____

_____

_____

ACTIVITY 20.4

LEADERSHIP IN ACTION

Aaliyah was in a group project where two of her teammates started arguing. Her first instinct was to jump in and pick a side. But instead, she stopped herself and thought, "If I just react, this gets worse. What's really going on here?"

She asked a few questions found out one person felt left out, so she suggested splitting the work more fairly. It wasn't perfect, but it calmed things down and helped them finish.

Aaliyah learned that leadership isn't about always having the smartest answer. Its about taking a moment to think, ask the right questions, and guide people toward a better solution.

REFLECTION TIME

- When did I use poor thinking, and what happened?

___

- Which type of thinking (analytical, creative, critical, reflective) do I use most?

___

- How could better thinking improve my leadership?

___

THINK ABOUT IT

1. Your group disagrees on how to finish a project. How do you use thinking skills to find a fair solution?

_____
_____

2. A friend dares you to do something risky. Do you react or reflect first?

_____
_____

3. You read something online that makes you mad. How can critical thinking help before you share it?

_____
_____

21

Vocational Foundations

Leading With Your Hands

Not All Leaders Wear Suits

When people think of leadership, they often imagine someone in an office, wearing a suit. But real leaders also fix cars, build houses, wire electricity, cut hair, cook meals, and keep communities running.

These are **vocational trades**—skilled jobs like electrician, mechanic, carpenter, plumber, chef, or welder. Leaders in trades use their skills, discipline, and teamwork to make life better for everyone.

What Counts as a Trade?

Trades are **hands-on** jobs where you build, repair, or create. They usually need training or certifications, but not always a college degree.

Office jobs (sometimes called "white-collar") often involve computers, paperwork, or management.

Both paths are valuable. The difference is in how you like to work.

Job Sort

Make two quick lists:

- List as many trades as you know.
- List as many office/white-collar jobs as you know.

Compare the two. Which list feels more interesting to you?

_____
_____
_____
_____

ACTIVITY 21.1

LEADERSHIP IN ACTION

Trades aren't "easy" jobs. They take serious leadership. Imagine being an electrician:

- You have to solve problems fast.
- You carry the responsibility of safety.
- You communicate with clients and teammates.
- You manage your time and deadlines.
- You keep learning new techniques.

That's leadership in action.

Skill Hunt

ACTIVITY 21.2

Pick one trade (like mechanic, carpenter, or chef). Write down **five leadership skills** someone in that trade needs. Example: reliability, communication, problem-solving.

Trade: _____

Leadership Skills:

_____

_____

_____

_____

_____

Trades vs. Office Jobs

Which is better? The truth: neither. The right choice depends on your personality, strengths, and goals.

- Office jobs may require more schooling.
- Trades may need hands-on training, certifications, or apprenticeships.
- Both can pay well and offer growth.
- Both need leadership.

> ### Mini Debate
>
> Write one reason why a trade job could be a great path. Then write one reason why an office job could be a great path.
>
> _____
> _____
> _____
> _____
>
> **ACTIVITY 21.3**

How to Prepare for a Trade Career

You don't have to wait until you're older. Teens can start preparing now by:

- Taking technical classes (math, science, shop, cooking, etc.).
- Building soft skills like punctuality and discipline.
- Volunteering for hands-on work.
- Asking about apprenticeships or certifications.

ACTIVITY 21.4

My Trade Path Checklist

Think of one trade you might consider. Write down one small step you can take this year to prepare (like practicing a skill, researching schools, or asking someone about their work).

_____
_____
_____
_____
_____
_____
_____

LEADERSHIP IN ACTION

Mohamed didn't think he was "smart enough" for college. But he loved fixing cars. He started helping at a local shop, got certified, and worked his way up. Now he runs his own auto repair business and teaches new workers.

His leadership isn't about a suit or office—it's about skill, responsibility, and guiding others.

REFLECTION TIME

- Would I consider a trade career? Why or why not?

- What strengths do I already have that could help in a trade job?

- What steps can I take this year to prepare for my future career?

THINK ABOUT IT

1. A family member says trades are "less important" than office jobs. How would you respond?

2. You're more hands-on than academic. How can a trade path turn that into strength?

3. A friend wants to start as a plumber, while you're looking at office work. How can you both respect each other's paths?

22

Performance
Turning Effort Into Results

Why Performance Matters

Leadership isn't just about good ideas—it's about results. You can talk all day about goals, but if nothing gets done, people stop listening.

Performance means **showing results that matter**. In school, that could mean finishing homework on time.

On a team, it could mean practicing hard and playing your role. In life, it means following through on what you say.

Effort vs. Results

Effort is important—you need to try. But effort alone isn't enough. Leaders check: Did my effort create results?
Example:

- Effort = running at practice.
- Result = being faster and ready for game day.

Effort and Results

Write down one thing you worked hard on. Then write down the result. Did the result match your effort? What would you do differently next time?

_____

_____

_____

_____

ACTIVITY 22.1

Performance is measured by outcomes. In school, it might be grades. In work, it could be tasks completed. In leadership, it's about trust—do people see you follow through?

How to Measure Performance

- **Completion** (Did you finish?).
- **Quality** (Did you do it well?).
- **Impact** (Did it make a difference?).

ACTIVITY 22.2

Success Check

Pick a past project (school, sports, or group activity). Write three ways you could measure its success (for example: attendance, improvement, positive feedback).

_____

_____

_____

_____

_____

Performance in Leadership

Leaders don't just start projects—they finish them. They hold themselves accountable. That means:

- Being consistent.
- Owning mistakes.
- Delivering what you promised.

Mini-Project Plan

Plan a small project (like a class game, a poster, or a group cleanup). Write down:

1. What is the goal?

_____
_____
_____

2. How will you measure success?

_____
_____
_____

3. Who will do what?

_____
_____
_____

ACTIVITY 22.3

Tools for Strong Performance

Leaders use tools to stay on track:

- **Checklists** keep you organized.
- **Peer feedback** shows you how others see your work.
- **Reflections** help you improve next time.

ACTIVITY 22.4

Create a Tracker

Choose one personal goal (like finishing a book, improving in sports, or saving money). Make a simple tracker with boxes you can check each time you make progress.

Personal Goal:

_____

Performance With Integrity

Some people fake results—cheating, lying, or cutting corners. That may look good for a moment, but it destroys trust. Real performance means being honest, even when results aren't perfect.

Scenario Talk

Imagine someone lies about their performance to look better. What happens when the truth comes out? Write down two possible consequences.

_____
_____
_____
_____
_____
_____

ACTIVITY 22.5

LEADERSHIP IN ACTION

You probably know the old story: the hare brags about how fast he is. The tortoise challenges him to a race. The hare takes off sprinting, then slows down, gets distracted, and even naps. The tortoise just keeps moving—slow, steady, focused. In the end, the tortoise wins. Not because he was faster, but because he **was consistent.**

Performance works the same way. You don't have to be the flashiest or the most talented. If you keep showing up, giving effort, and finishing strong, people will trust you more than someone who burns bright for a moment and disappears.

REFLECTION TIME

- What does good performance mean to me?

  _____
  _____
  _____

- What gets in the way of me performing at my best?

  _____
  _____
  _____

- How can I measure my progress without comparing myself to others?

  _____
  _____
  _____

THINK ABOUT IT

1. You promise to help with a project but forget to show up. How do you repair your performance?

   _____
   _____
   _____
   _____

THINK ABOUT IT CONTINUE

2. A teammate does less work but takes all the credit. How should you handle it?

_____

_____

_____

3. You're not getting the results you want even though you're trying hard. What's your next step?

_____

_____

_____

I Can Lead
My Leadership Legacy

Looking Back—and Ahead

Pause for a moment. Take a breath. Think about the first page of this book. When you started, the word **leader** might have felt distant—maybe you pictured a president, a famous speaker, or someone with a microphone. Now you've learned something important: leadership begins on the inside. It's in your thoughts, words, and choices. Every small act of courage, kindness, and responsibility makes you a leader.

So, what comes next?

Your Leadership Legacy

Your **legacy** is what people remember about you—the mark you leave on the world. It doesn't have to be huge. A legacy could be:

- The friend who always listens.
- The sibling who stands up for fairness.
- The classmate who includes others.
- The person who looks for solutions instead of complaining.
- The neighbor who volunteers to help out.

All of these are legacies. They show how your leadership keeps making the world better, even when you're not around.

What Will Yours Be?

Imagine a friend or family member talking about you in the future. What would you want them to say? Complete these sentences in your own words:

- "They were the kind of person who …"
- "People felt … when they were around them."
- "They always tried to …"

These sentences are pieces of your leadership legacy.

A Quick Leadership Legacy Activity

"I want to be a leader who inspires hope in others, so that people never give up on their dreams.

1. Fold a piece of paper in half.
2. On the left side, write "Who I Am Now" and list three to five qualities or habits you see in yourself as a leader.
3. On the right side, write **"My Leadership Legacy"** and list three to five ways you'd like to grow as a leader.
4. Pick one thing from the right side to work on this week.

Remember: You're Already Leading

You don't have to wait until you're older, richer, or more well-known. You are already making a difference. You have ideas worth sharing, values worth standing up for, and a heart that wants to do good. That's what true leadership is.

So go out there and lead. The world needs your light. Say it with confidence:

I CAN LEAD.

My Legacy Story

1. Think of someone you admire. It could be a friend, teacher, or someone in history. What is their legacy?
2. Now think about your own future. What do you want to be remembered for?
3. Write 3-5 sentences describing what you would say about yourself five years from now if you live up to your potential.

_____

_____

_____

_____

ACTIVITY 23.1

Legacy Brainstorm

1. List three small actions you can take this week that match the legacy you want to build. For example, helping a younger student with homework, standing up for someone, or creating a positive post online.
2. Commit to doing at least one of them and write about how it went.

_____

_____

_____

_____

ACTIVITY 23.2

My Leadership Legacy Statement

Use the structure below to write your own Leadership Legacy Statement. Put it somewhere you'll see it often—like on your desk or in your journal.

"I want to be a leader who [action/quality], so that [impact]. I will do this by [how you'll act]."

Example:

"I want to be a leader who inspires hope in others, so that people never give up on their dreams. I will do this by encouraging people, sharing good ideas, and helping solve problems."

_____
_____
_____
_____

ACTIVITY 23.3

References

Glossary of Key Terms

Below are some important terms from **I Can Lead** and what they mean. Use this page as a quick reference to remind yourself of the concepts you've learned.

Term	Simple Definition
Accountability	Owning your actions and their results, good or bad.
Adaptability	Adjusting when things change instead of breaking down.
Anger Management	Tools and habits to keep your cool instead of lashing out.
Authority	A person, rule, or system you need to follow (like parents, teachers, or laws).
Balance	Keeping school, family, rest, and fun steady — not letting one take over.
Boundaries	Limits you set to protect your time, energy, and values.
Choices	The decisions you make every day that shape your future.
Communication	How you share your thoughts, feelings, and needs with others.
Compassion	Caring about other people and wanting to help them.
Consistency	Showing up and doing the right thing again and again, not just once.

Term	Simple Definition
Courage	Doing the right thing even when it's hard or scary.
Critical Thinking	Slowing down to question things and make smarter choices.
Decision-Making	The process of choosing between different options.
Discipline	Training yourself to stay focused, follow rules, and not give up.
Empathy	Putting yourself in someone else's shoes and trying to feel what they feel.
Fairness	Treating people equally and giving everyone a fair chance.
Forgiveness	Letting go of anger or grudges so you can move forward.
Goals	Specific results you want to reach (short-term or long-term).
Grit	Sticking with something even when it's really tough.
Growth Mindset	Believing you can get better at something if you keep trying.
Identity	Who you are on the inside: your values, personality, and what matters to you.
Innovation	Finding a new or creative way to solve a problem.
Integrity	Being real and honest, even when no one is watching.
Justice	Making sure people's rights are respected and wrongs are made right.
Leadership	Helping yourself and others move in a positive direction.

Term	Simple Definition
Legacy	The impact or memory you leave behind when people think of you.
Mission	What you want your life to be about — the main path you're walking.
Obligations	Responsibilities or duties you have (like schoolwork, family, or promises).
Obstacles	Things that block your path but can be worked around.
Patience	Staying calm and steady, even when things take time.
Performance	Turning your effort into real results people can count on.
Perseverance	Keeping at something, even when it's tough.
Purpose	The reason why you do what you do.
Reflection	Taking time to think back on what happened and what you learned.
Resilience	The ability to bounce back after setbacks or mistakes.
Respect	Treating people in a way that shows they matter.
Responsibility	Taking care of what's yours and owning your actions.
Rights	The basic things every human deserves (like safety, respect, and freedom of thought).
Role Model	Someone whose behavior you look up to and can learn from.
Self-Awareness	Knowing your own feelings, strengths, and weak spots.

Term	Simple Definition
Self-Control	Stopping yourself from acting on impulse or anger.
Strategy	A plan for how you'll reach a goal or solve a problem.
Submission	Choosing to follow higher values, role models, or laws that guide you.
Teamwork	Working well with others toward a goal.
Trade / Vocational Path	Hands-on jobs like mechanic, cook, barber, or construction worker.
Values	The beliefs or rules that guide what you do.
Vision	The picture of your future you want to build.

References & Inspirations

Emotional Intelligence Training Company. (2023). **How to Improve Emotional Intelligence in the Workplace**. Retrieved from https://www.eitrainingcompany.com

Nassar, Ayman and Nisar, Zain, "**Acing My Game: Self-awareness**", I Can Lead Empowered, 2023 Youth Summer Empowerment Program for Mayor's Office on Neighborhood Safety and Engagement (MONSE), Islamic Leadership Institute of America, June 2023.

Nassar, Ayman and Nisar, Zain, "**Fine Line Between Courage & Stupidity: Risk Analysis & Smart Choice**", I Can Lead Empowered, 2023 Youth Summer Empowerment Program for Mayor's Office on Neighborhood Safety and Engagement (MONSE), Islamic Leadership Institute of America, June 2023.

Nassar, Ayman and Nisar, Zain, "**My Map to the Future: Vision**", I Can Lead Empowered, 2023 Youth Summer Empowerment Program for Mayor's Office on Neighborhood Safety and Engagement (MONSE), Islamic Leadership Institute of America, June 2023.

Nassar, Ayman and Nisar, Zain, "**Make the Click, Bridge the Gap: Communicating with Adults**", I Can Lead Empowered, 2023 Youth Summer Empowerment Program for Mayor's Office on Neighborhood Safety and Engagement (MONSE), Islamic Leadership Institute of America, June 2023.

Nassar, Ayman and Nisar, Zain, "*My World: Rights and Obligations*", I Can Lead Empowered, 2023 Youth Summer Empowerment Program for Mayor's Office on Neighborhood Safety and Engagement (MONSE), Islamic Leadership Institute of America, June 2023.

Nassar, Ayman and Nisar, Zain, "*Patience, Perseverance and Steadfastness*", I Can Lead Empowered, 2023 Youth Summer Empowerment Program for Mayor's Office on Neighborhood Safety and Engagement (MONSE), Islamic Leadership Institute of America, June 2023.

Nassar, Ayman and Nisar, Zain, "*Problem Solving for Teens and Young Adults*", I Can Lead Empowered, 2023 Youth Summer Empowerment Program for Mayor's Office on Neighborhood Safety and Engagement (MONSE), Islamic Leadership Institute of America, June 2023.

Nassar, Ayman and Nisar, Zain, "*What am I all About: Mission & Purpose*", I Can Lead Empowered, 2023 Youth Summer Empowerment Program for Mayor's Office on Neighborhood Safety and Engagement (MONSE), Islamic Leadership Institute of America, June 2023.

Nassar, Ayman and Nisar, Zain, "*Who am I: Identity Building*", I Can Lead Empowered, 2023 Youth Summer Empowerment Program for Mayor's Office on Neighborhood Safety and Engagement (MONSE), Islamic Leadership Institute of America, May 2023.

Nassar, Ayman and Nisar, Zain, "*Smart Hustle: Time Management*", I Can Lead Empowered, 2023 Youth Summer Empowerment Program for Mayor's Office on Neighborhood Safety and Engagement (MONSE), Islamic Leadership Institute of America, June 2023.

Nassar, Ayman, "*Identity, Submission and Islam*", Friday Khutbah at Maryum Islamic Center, Woodbine, Maryland, YouTube, https://www.youtube.com/watch?v=FUxBB0goEYM, March 4th, 2022.

Nassar, Ayman, "***Mountain Strong: Patience in Practice***", Islamic Leadership Institute of America, August 2009.

Nassar, Ayman, "***Youth Challenges, Root Causes & Tips for Parents***", Islamic Leadership Institute of America, June 2015.

Index of Topics, Skills & Concepts

Accountability, 151–154
 Taking ownership, 151
 Learning from mistakes, 154
Adaptability, 19–24, 155–157
 Adjusting to change, 20
 Staying flexible, 156
Ambition, 27–31
 Setting goals, 28
 Staying motivated, 31
Anger Management, 96–99
 Identifying triggers, 96
 Calming strategies, 97
 Controlling reactions, 98
Authority, 67–69
 Following laws and rules, 68
 Respecting leadership, 69
Balance, 55–66
 Managing time, 56
 Staying organized, 58
Biography, 31
 Defining, 31
Boundaries, 87–95
 Emotional boundaries, 88
 Respecting personal space, 80
Bravery, 27–33, 100–107
 Courage vs. impulse, 101
 Standing up for what's right, 103
Career Readiness, 146–148, 184-186
 Job skills, 149
 Resume writing, 184
Character Building, 67–74
 Submission, 68
 Purification, 72

Choices, 100–114
Consequences, 101
Smart decisions, 104

Communication, 75–85
Asking for help, 78
Listening skills, 80
Speaking respectfully, 81
Feedback, 83

Community, 109–114, 146–148
Service, 110
Citizenship, 149

Compassion, 50–54, 109–114
Caring for others, 51
Empathy, 112

Confidence, 19–34
Building self-belief, 20
Overcoming fear, 34

Conflict Resolution, 75–85, 96–99
Staying calm, 97
Listening to understand, 81

Consistency, 50–54, 151–154
Keeping routines, 52
Following through, 154

Cooperation, 40–49, 146–148
Working in teams, 42
Respecting roles, 147

Courage, 27–33, 100–107
Making bold choices, 102
Doing right even when hard, 104

Creativity, 40–49, 140–144
Brainstorming, 42
Problem-solving, 143

Critical Thinking, 40–49, 140–144
Asking questions, 40
Evaluating options, 143

Decision-Making, 40–49, 100–107
Weighing choices, 102
Learning from results, 106

Determination, 50–54, 153-156
Sticking with it, 53
Finishing strong, 155

Discipline, 55–69
Focus, 56
Self-control, 67
Diversity, 75–85, 109–114
Inclusion, 110
Respecting differences, 78
Emotional Awareness, 87–99
Recognizing feelings, 88
Managing emotions, 93
Empathy, 109–114
Seeing from others' view, 110
Responding with care, 112
Ethics, 71–74, 120–122
Doing what's right, 73
Being fair, 121
Failure, 34–54, 133–137
Learning from mistakes, 36
Bouncing back, 135
Fairness, 120–122
Equal treatment, 120
Just decisions, 121
Faith & Values, 27–33, 67–69
Believing in purpose, 28
Following higher principles, 68
Focus, 55–66, 133–137
Staying on task, 57
Avoiding distractions, 134
Forgiveness, 50–54, 87–95
Letting go, 53
Moving forward, 93
Friendship, 75–78
Building trust, 76
Communication, 77
Generosity, 116–118
Giving back, 117
Helping others, 118
Goal-Setting, 34–40, 151–154
Short-term goals, 36
Long-term vision, 153
Gratitude, 27–33, 50–54
Appreciating blessings, 29
Showing thanks, 50

Growth Mindset, 133–137
Learning from challenges, 135
Staying curious, 134

Honesty, 19–24, 120–122
Telling the truth, 20
Keeping integrity, 121

Hope, 34–54
Staying positive, 35
Seeing possibilities, 37

Humility, 157–160
Accepting feedback, 158
Lifting others up, 160

Identity, 19–25
Who am I?, 21
Role models, 24

Imagination, 34–49
Seeing possibilities, 35
Creating new ideas, 48

Integrity, 71–74, 153–155
Doing the right thing, 72
Being dependable, 155

Justice, 160-164
Standing for what's right, 160
Protecting others' rights, 161

Kindness, 79–85, 109–114
Helping others, 80
Treating people gently, 112

Leadership, 20–23, 146–150
Self-leadership, 21
Leading others, 148

Legacy, 160–163
What you leave behind, 160
How you'll be remembered, 162

Learning, 133–137
Growing through mistakes, 134
Applying knowledge, 135

Listening, 75–85, 94–98
Paying attention, 81
Understanding others, 96

Loyalty, 19–25, 120–122
Staying true, 21
Standing by your people, 121

Mindset, 50–54, 133–137
- *Positive thinking, 53*
- *Growth attitude, 137*

Motivation, 34–37, 151–157
- *Finding your "why," 35*
- *Pushing through, 155*

Obedience, 67–69
- *Following guidance, 68*
- *Respecting boundaries, 69*

Obligations, 109–114
- *Responsibilities, 110*
- *Doing your part, 112*

Opportunity, 34–38, 151–157
- *Taking initiative, 36*
- *Making smart moves, 155*

Organization, 40–49, 55–66
- *Planning ahead, 42*
- *Managing priorities, 58*

Patience, 50–54, 116–118
- *Waiting calmly, 51*
- *Staying steady, 117*

Performance, 151–157
- *Results that matter, 154*
- *Accountability, 155*

Personal Growth, 19–25, 133–137
- *Learning about yourself, 20*
- *Improving daily, 135*

Planning, 34–37, 55–66
- *Making a plan, 35*
- *Following through, 58*

Problem-Solving, 40–49
- *Finding solutions, 42*
- *Thinking critically, 46*

Purpose, 27–37
- *Mission in life, 28*
- *Doing what matters, 31*

Purification, 71–74
- *Cleansing habits, 72*
- *Building good character, 73*

Reflection, 151–157
- *Journaling, 155*
- *Self-check, 151*

Relationships, 79–85, 109–116
　Family communication, 80
　Respect and empathy, 115
Resilience, 50–54, 133–135
　Bouncing back, 51
　Growing stronger, 134
Respect, 75–85
　Showing regard, 83
　Listening without judgment, 80
Responsibility, 109–114, 124–131
　Taking charge, 112
　Doing your duty, 126
Risk-Taking, 100–107
　Courage with wisdom, 102
　Smart choices, 104
Role Models, 19–25, 67–69
　Learning from others, 24
　Following examples, 67
Sacrifice, 67–69, 157–159
　Giving up for good, 67
　Leading with service, 158
Self-Awareness, 87–95
　Knowing yourself, 88
　Recognizing emotions, 94
Self-Control, 67–69, 96–99
　Managing reactions, 68
　Staying calm, 98
Self-Discipline, 55–69
　Staying on track, 56
　Following routines, 67
Self-Respect, 19–25, 75–85
　Valuing yourself, 21
　Setting limits, 80
Service, 109–114, 146–150
　Giving time, 110
　Helping community, 149
Strength, 50–54, 96–99
　Power under control, 97
　Inner toughness, 52
Stress Management, 55–66, 96–99
　Breathing techniques, 97
　Time balance, 57

Teamwork, 40–49, 146–150
  Collaboration, 42
  Shared goals, 149
Time Management, 55–66
  Scheduling, 56
  Avoiding procrastination, 59
Trade Skills, 146–150
  Working with hands, 148
  Leadership in trades, 150
Trust, 19–25, 157–159
  Earning respect, 21
  Keeping promises, 160
Values, 19–25, 27–33, 67–69
  Moral compass, 28
  What guides you, 67
Vision, 34–40
  Seeing your future, 36
  Mapping goals, 39
Wealth, 116–118
  Resources and money, 117
  Giving back, 118
Work Ethic, 146–155
  Doing your best, 149
  Being dependable, 155

Services for Youth Ages 14-24

1. Youth Leadership Development

Learn by doing, build meaningful connections, and lead change in your community. We help unlock the leader in you.

2. Youth Career Empowerment

A stepping stone to your future, helping you build goals and unlock your potential early.

3. Youth Wellness & Stabilization

A supportive space for youth to reset, grow stronger, and work on their next level.

4. Youth Advocacy & Inclusion

Learn about real-world issues, take action, and make impact with support from a mentor.

Want to join all four youth programs? We got you! Contact us in one of details below to get you started.

Website: islamicleadership.org

Email: icanlead@islamicleadership.org

Juvenile Active Learning Framework

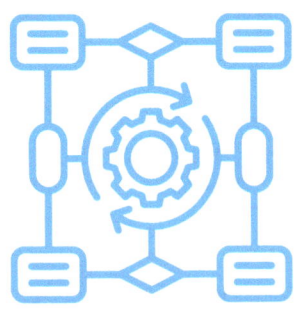

In ILIA, the youth are treated as developing leaders capable of taking responsibilities and managing choices. Our Juvenile Active Learning (JAL) Framework is designed to support resource limited environments by strengthening decision making skills in a leadership-centered approach.

JAL adopts the David P. Weikart Center for Youth Program Quality (CYPQ) applied under conditions of trauma, constraint, and with an Islamic perspective aligned to ILIA's Positive Youth Development Program to serve youth of all backgrounds.

Visit at **pyd.islamicleadership.org** to read more

Teachers Professional Development Training

Teachers shape the leadership of every generation. Not only do they provide inspiration to our youth, but also for the future that is yet to come.

ILIA offers eight (8) Educational Units for teachers to receive a certificate in Classroom Leadership with the following coursework:

- Turning the Chaos into Memorable Experiences
- Building Young Leaders in Your Classroom
- Make the Click, Bridge the Gap
- Teaching ADHD Youth

Interested? Contact ss@islamicleadership.org for more details.

Made in the USA
Columbia, SC
22 February 2026